STEPHEN POWELL is a journalist who worked for Reuters for twenty-seven years. He has lived and worked on every continent except Antarctica and brings to his craft a deeply ingrained global perspective. His reporting has included war and coups in Africa and Brazil's transition from military rule to democracy. He lives in the Brecon Beacons, in the town of Crickhowell.

THE FIRST TOAST IS TO PEACE

TRAVELS IN THE SOUTH CAUCASUS

STEPHEN POWELL

SilverWood

Published in 2018 by SilverWood Books

SilverWood Books Ltd
14 Small Street, Bristol, BS1 1DE, United Kingdom
www.silverwoodbooks.co.uk

ISBN 978-1-78132-725-8 (paperback)
ISBN 978-1-78132-809-5 (ebook)

British Library Cataloguing in Publication Data
A CIP catalogue record for this book is available from the British Library

Page design and typesetting by SilverWood Books
Printed on responsibly sourced paper

To my Mum and Dad who first gave me a taste for foreign travel

Contents

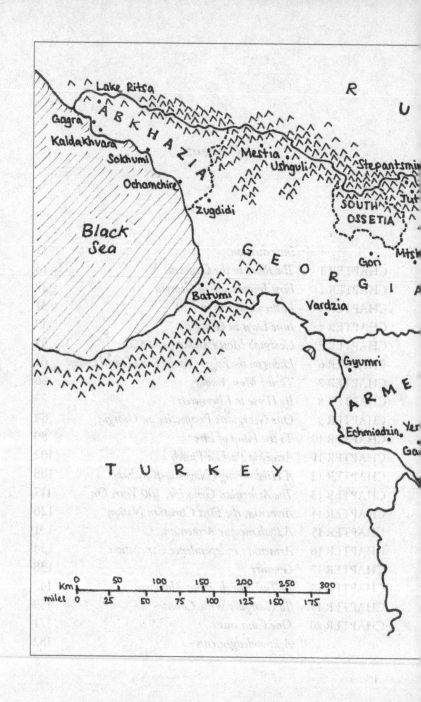

S I A

tili
Darlo
alo
elavi

Sighnaghi
Gareji

Sudur

Qirmizi
Qesebe

Caspian
Sea

A Z E R B A I J A N

Vank

NAGORNO
KARABAKH

Shushi Stepanakert

Toghi Hadrut

Baku

Meghri

R A N

Introduction

The Caucasus summoned me and I obeyed. The idea of heading to this spectacular region, where I knew no one and had never set foot, first gripped my imagination early in 2014. It came out of a clear blue sky. A very old friend took a holiday in Georgia and this triggered the most intense emotion within me – I wanted to go there too!

That was the whole decision-making process, as simple and baffling as that. I opted to set out the following spring. I had recently done some major decluttering, selling a twenty-four-hectare smallholding on a Welsh hillside, plus my car, all in the same week. I felt gloriously lighter, in a perfect frame of mind to contemplate some extended foreign travel.

The majestic landscape and the turbulent history of the South Caucasus, caught between Russia to the north and Muslim Turkey and Iran to the south, seemed like it might provide the stuff of an absorbing adventure.

As I approached my sixty-fifth birthday, a journey to one of the great mountain ranges of the world appealed far more than golf or gardening.

My aims were to try to capture the spirit of the place and its peoples and simply to enjoy a part of the world wholly new to me.

I would travel and write largely for my own satisfaction. I was, after all, bringing together two lifelong passions.

But as 2014 unfolded, with Russia's seizure of Ukraine's Crimea and conflict in eastern Ukraine, I became aware of another reason for going to the Caucasus. One major factor in the Ukraine fighting was clear Russian support for the rebels and it seemed to me that the world was witnessing Russia in the role of bully. An idea formed in my mind that the more the outside world knew about the former Soviet republics, the more they were 'real' places in people's heads, the better placed they might be to keep Russia at bay. This could be a deluded view, but it played a part in my thinking and I offer this account of my travels in three former Soviet republics in the conviction that they deserve support in their new-found independence and deserve to be better understood.

In the end I went to the South Caucasus four times, three times in 2015 and then again in the summer of 2016. In all I spent nearly half a year in the region. As I moved around I kept a travel blog, partly to guard against the possibility of losing my notes, so what follows builds on my contemporaneous accounts.

CHAPTER 1

The Road to the Caucasus

Preparation for the journey was fun and varied. I was flexible about modes of transport in the Caucasus, but surely slow is good when exploring an unfamiliar region. So the preparation included horse-riding, to see whether I still had any of the equestrian skills acquired in my youth.

With my old friend Suzie Greenwood, in March 2015 I flew to the Azores, out there on the Mid-Atlantic Ridge, for a week's riding.

Rodrigo, from Braga in mainland Portugal, assessed our riding ability in a *picadeiro*, an outdoor riding arena.

Evidently we passed muster. In guided groups we went out on horseback on six consecutive days, riding through the hills and vales of São Miguel, the main Azorean island. I rode a different horse every day, climbing into the saddle on Zoria, Capitão, Universo, Cabana, Zarita and Flor.

The jewel in the crown was our ride on the last day, not far from the western tip of São Miguel. We set off on a twenty-five-kilometre ride in bright sunshine. "When angels travel the sun always shines," said one of my fellow riders, Monika from Aachen, as she helped to adjust my saddle.

We began the ride with a ridge of steep wooded hill ahead of us at right angles to our path. We turned to our right at a tarmac road and then left onto a dirt track. "It is a little steep on the left," said Rodrigo our guide, referring to an incline at that point hidden from view.

But it soon became clear that we were riding along the rim of an ancient volcano, with a crater down on our left. Two glorious lakes gradually came into view at the bottom, Lagoa Verde and Lagoa Azul.

To complete the picture, on our right, past a patchwork quilt of fields, conifer woodlands and villages with red-tiled roofs, was the Atlantic Ocean, less than four kilometres away. It all built up to a sensation of the world as scenic idyll.

We led our horses down a steep track to the crater bottom and after a ride through farmland with cows grazing, we picnicked on the bank of the smaller lake, Lagoa Verde. After lunch we enjoyed several canters, on tracks skirting both of the lakes.

A great week! And the learning? The trip reminded me that travelling by horse through beautiful countryside is one of life's great experiences. I learned that I could still ride. A horse or a mule could be an option for part of the Caucasus odyssey.

After the horse ride came a very different type of preparation. I flew from London to Riga, the Latvian capital, for two weeks in the classroom working on my Russian. A quarter of a century after the end of the Soviet Union, Russian is still the *lingua franca* of the Caucasus.

I started to study Russian about the time of the Beatles' first LP. A programme appeared on British television, with an avuncular male presenter helping viewers to learn the basics of the language. I was hooked. More than half a century later I can still remember some of the phrases he taught.

Город стоит на холме. The town stands on a hill.

Я играю на гитаре. I play the guitar.

Time and again over the decades the language and the culture have drawn me back. Frankly, it can be a relief to return to Russian after Welsh, the indigenous language of my native land. Educators in Wales have a habit of producing two sets of language textbooks for adult learners – one set for South Wales and another for the slightly different speech of the north.

Now you can fit Wales into the territory of the Russian Federation more than 800 times, but Russian educators take a firm linguistic line. They have no truck with regional nuances and produce textbooks conveying the message, "In Russian we say it like this." For the harassed learner, the thwack of Muscovite command has much to commend it.

In Riga you constantly hear Russian and the city has a very professional language school in the Education Centre DURBE. All in all, over two visits in 2014 and 2015, I spent three weeks in its classrooms.

The experience of Riga opened up a whole world. The physical landscape of the Baltic states is flat and rather featureless, but the human and linguistic contours in this part of Europe are fascinating.

About a third of Latvia's two million people are Russian speakers, but the only official language is Latvian. The narrative that runs in the heads of many Latvian speakers is not the same as the narrative that holds sway for the Russian speakers.

Vladimir Putin famously called the dissolution of the Soviet Union "the greatest geopolitical catastrophe of the twentieth century". This is the point of view of the president of Russia and not everyone shares it. But the least one can say is that the demise of the USSR took away a whole framework, an emotional, practical context, for the lives of millions of people.

Studying Russian at DURBE on my second visit, I stayed in the home of a middle-aged Russian speaker, Lyudmila, an attentive and kindly host. She was born and raised in the city of Murmansk, in the extreme northwest of Russia above the Arctic Circle. She studied in the city that for her will always be Leningrad, not St. Petersburg. In my bedroom the most prominent book on the shelves was *Soviet Latvia*.

Over a breakfast of porridge on 22 April, Lyudmila said to me, "Today is Lenin's birthday. This was a big holiday in the Soviet Union."

It is human to feel nostalgia. But there can be real practical difficulties for the Russian speakers who lived to see the end of the Soviet Union, which included Latvia and the other two Baltic states, Estonia and Lithuania. Lyudmila's brother still lives in Murmansk and since she is now a Latvian citizen she needs a visa simply to go and see him.

Russian speakers tend to watch Moscow television and to socialise out of work with other Russian speakers. Their points of reference are to the east. Latvian speakers, on the other hand, mix with Latvian speakers and their points of reference are to the west. For them, Russia has again and again appeared in the historical role of invader. During the Soviet period, Moscow brought to the Baltic states the whole Stalinist toolkit of deportations, torture and murder.

In 2014, during my first visit to the language school, the Latvians opened up to visitors the former KGB headquarters in central Riga, a sinister building on Brivibas Iela, or Freedom Street. It was here on Freedom Street that KGB men shot dead Latvian 'enemies', running engines to mask the sound of gunfire.

Latvia has moved quickly to integrate itself into the European Union and NATO. For Latvian speakers, the Soviet period was a dark time and they want a very different future. Memories of the Soviet past are still very raw, as I realised when I met Indra Mangule, a feisty young Latvian woman working in Riga.

When I met her, Indra had spent five years in Britain, studying in Glasgow and London. Her English is faultless and she lives and breathes a spirit of alignment with Europe. She remembers vividly what it was like, as a child, to live through the failed Soviet coup of August 1991 when conspirators sought to overthrow Soviet leader Mikhail Gorbachev. Shockwaves went out through the whole crumbling edifice of the Soviet Union.

Indra, in Riga with her mother at the time, said to me, "I remember seeing a tank, seeing soldiers." She also remembered her mother keeping an axe under a bed. Years later she asked her mother, "Why the axe?"

"Well, I would have chopped them up," said Indra's mother, referring to the reception that would have greeted any Russian soldiers coming to their home.

Since Russia's seizure of Ukraine's Crimea in 2014 there has been an edginess in the Baltic states, which constitute NATO's eastern flank.

For the language school DURBE, the new tensions between Russia and the West are a business opportunity. They began running specialist courses on Russian terms for military technology. The United States Air Force is one of their clients. Lyudmila, a lover of the Russian classics, has hosted a USAF officer, who told her that Russian was a strategic language. I wish I had been a fly on the wall for some of their conversations!

In Riga, Georgia started to make its presence felt. Along with my Australian godson Tom, who came to see the city, I went to listen to one of Georgia's leading singers, Nino Katamadze. She is a big-hearted woman with a voice to match. She and her band played some very high-energy music, more or less of the jazz persuasion, to a full house at the Riga Congress Centre.

In the Latvian capital, Georgia just happened to be the one country that really stood out in terms of advertising its charms as a travel destination. From billboards sprang the words *Vasara Gruzija* (Summer in Georgia) and an enticing image of a lake, a hotel and wooded hills. All of this put me in a very Georgian frame of mind.

After my Russian lessons were done, I went overland from the Baltic shore to Georgia, to feel the vibes of the places in between and to flex my traveller muscles. Roughly the first third of the journey was the road to Ukraine.

I made a start with the night bus from Riga to Warsaw, which offered hot meals to passengers and was most comfortable. Just as well, since this was a twelve-hour bus ride.

We rolled into Warsaw shortly after 5am. I had been to Warsaw before, but I marvelled afresh at the hum and modernity of this thrusting city, at the monumental scale of reconstruction. In 1945 this was one of two national capitals destroyed by war, the other being Manila. What work the Poles have done.

Within minutes I was heading south on a train to Kraków, capital of Poland from 1038 to 1569, and by any measure one of Europe's architectural jewels. I had been here too in the past and again I was struck on arrival by the sheer energy of the place.

I checked into a hostel in the city's former Jewish district Kazimierz, dotted with a multitude of bars, restaurants and clubs. Looking about me, I decided that Kraków must be competing for the title of party capital of Europe.

South of Kraków lie the Tatra Mountains and the trick was to choose a public transport option that got me to Slovakia on the other side of the range. I started with a bus to Katowice, where I spotted the first working coal mine I had seen in years.

Then a train from Katowice to the Slovakian town of Žilina, where I changed train for Košice. From Žilina to Košice was a lovely ride, with the snow-capped Tatra now to the north. We passed a succession of picturesque towns and villages with many wooden houses. Slovakia looked very cosy.

I read a short story by Chekhov, *The Lady with a Dog*, and told myself, "This is the life."

I arrived in Košice, Slovakia's second city, on a Monday evening and it was a shock after Kraków. Košice was deadly quiet. The only person out in the streets near the city's fourteenth-century Gothic cathedral turned out to be a statue.

Košice is a city of substance with a long history. The Bradt Travel Guide says it was the first in Europe to be awarded a municipal coat of arms, in 1369.

On arrival at a hostel the receptionist kindly offered me a free vegan dinner, as part of the deal for guests. Having just dined I demurred and negotiated two free beers instead.

The next stage of the journey was to Uzhhorod in western Ukraine. I travelled by bus with a midwife from Seattle of Welsh extraction whom I had met at the hostel. We were the only Western tourists heading into Ukraine on this particular vehicle.

The border formalities to leave Slovakia and enter Ukraine took an hour. The female Ukrainian border guard who came onto our bus to collect our passports was dressed in military fatigues.

Uzhhorod is not prospering; that was immediately apparent. Of course, with fighting in eastern Ukraine making world headlines for the previous year and claiming more than 6,000 lives, visitors to the country are thin on the ground.

It felt as if time had stood still in the town for a generation. Some of the street signage, like an Intourist sign for a hotel, appeared to go back to Soviet times. Walking down one street, I passed a woman with a beaten-up old pram scavenging in rubbish bins. A few metres further on, another woman was selling meagre quantities of radishes, spring onions and other vegetables laid out on the pavement.

The town, once part of the Austro-Hungarian empire, has its charms, in particular a magnificent medieval castle ruled for centuries by counts of Franco-Italian origin. In a happier land, the trippers would be checking it out.

In the evening I took a stroll with Lynn, the Seattle midwife, and we discovered that the beating heart of Uzhhorod at night is by the Uzh river. At a café along the riverbank we had a dessert, coffee and a nightcap. The café offered blankets to customers feeling the chill of the night and the young waitress who served us was the very soul of friendliness.

"Where are you from?" she asked with genuine curiosity shining in her face. We talked a bit and she said she was a student.

"What are you studying?" I asked. "Tourism," she said, giving us a smile to melt the heart.

The next country on my itinerary was Romania. After one night in Uzhhorod, I set off on 29 April on a wheezing, crowded country bus that would take me to a border town.

We passed a succession of Ukrainian villages set back from the road which somehow were neither picturesque nor ugly, all dominated by tall churches often painted a pale yellow. During a journey of 170 kilometres, I observed a densely populated rural area, but its way of life was a closed book. The Carpathian Mountains formed a backdrop to the villages.

I left the bus at the border town of Solotvyno, or rather just after it because I had not realised where we were. Solotvyno has been known historically for its salt mines. It was also the birthplace of the late British press baron Robert Maxwell and at that time belonged to Czechoslovakia.

A walk of about ninety minutes took me to the border post. Now border crossings can be a time-consuming bore, but this one was delightful.

The border is on the Tisza river and after completing formalities on the Ukrainian side I simply walked across a short bridge to Romania, to its region of Transylvania. According to Hitchwiki, the hitchhiker's guide to hitching the world, this is the only border crossing between Ukraine and Romania where travellers are allowed to cross on foot.

After Ukraine I felt I was entering a land of milk and honey. I checked into a rather grand-looking hotel, the first that came into view, and found a comfortable bed for a modest price.

I was in Sighetu Marmaţiei and a bustling town it was too. Waiting at a bus stop the next day I was reminded that for many Romanians this is not a land of milk and honey. Stickers on buses advertised rides to Belgium (€80) and England (£70). The listed destinations included the London suburbs of Wood Green, Neasden and Wembley. I had not expected in Transylvania to find ads enticing me to Neasden. I ignored the ads and stuck to my plan of travelling to Cluj-Napoca, unofficial capital of Transylvania and the second most populous city of Romania.

The bus ride to Cluj was enchanting. Unlike the road in Ukraine this one went straight through villages. We travelled through one settlement after another for hours and now I did get a sense of how local people lived.

I was travelling in twenty-first-century Europe through a region where traditional subsistence farming and local craft appeared to be alive and well. We passed literally hundreds of houses with backyards full of hens. Often the houses had intricately carved high wooden gates at the front.

Now, while I accept that one backyard with hens looks much

like another, the overall visual stimulus in a peasant society, if you are not from one yourself, is extraordinary. There was much to see – a woman washing laundry in a river, a man ploughing with a horse, a family filling a mixer with cement, shepherds minding their flocks.

The most memorable sight was of two women in headscarves chatting and walking side by side in the early evening with hoes slung over their shoulders. For me, it was the visual equivalent of great poetry, something so simple in its essence that it touched the core of my being. It spoke to me of harmony, companionship and timeless rhythms on the earth. This simple message of connectedness, to one another and to the planet, made my heart sing. Since the hoe goes back to antiquity, at least to ancient Sumer, I was looking at a scene which could have existed 5,000 years ago.

If the two women ever read this, they will shake their heads in bewilderment or crack their sides with laughter. But I know that it is for experiences like this that the traveller leaves home in the first place. So often it is the little things that make the biggest impact.

At Cluj I stayed three nights, to rest and to absorb Romania by osmosis. Cluj is a handsome city, full of life and character, with a history and an architecture that are largely Hungarian.

For the ten-hour journey from Cluj to Bucharest I took the train, partly to follow the example of Prince Yakimov, the character in Olivia Manning's *The Balkan Trilogy*, who travels the self-same route. In his case, the fictional train journey takes place in wartime and is shot through with menace.

In my case there was no sense of menace, though I did well to stock up with water and a sandwich since there was no buffet car. I also bought a copy of the *Transilvania Reporter*, a local weekly. I have no Romanian but I couldn't resist the title.

At times during the journey, such as near the town of Sinaia, the Carpathians are quite magnificent, their peaks rising sharply and filling much of the view out of the train window.

Finally we drew into Bucharest. The city is clearly a whole world unto itself and I stayed only two nights. But I was charmed to find that it has leafy cycle paths. Why was I so surprised by this? Sometimes travel says a lot about our own preconceptions.

Because I was travelling by train and staying in hostels, I met a lot of young Romanians. One theme came up again and again in conversation. Students and even youngsters who were now working told me that their parents regularly sent them food parcels.

In Bucharest, Paula Posea, whom I met in my hostel, talked to me about this phenomenon. She did a food technology course in the capital and every term-time weekend for four years her parents sent her food. It came by bus from her parents' town nearly 200 kilometres away.

The food included milk from her own cow, which was still with her parents, eggs from their own hens, home-made fruit preserves, pork fat called *slanina* and a full soup known as *ciorbă*.

"But the most important thing in every package," said Paula, "is *zacuscă*, made from aubergines and some other ingredients like red pepper." Typically it is eaten spread over bread.

Several students said that without these food parcels it would be hard for them to make ends meet, but this living tradition also says a lot about the importance of both food and family in Romania.

When I asked Paula, "Why the food parcels?" she said, "Romanians like to eat, end of story. So the food you grow up with is very important. I can't stay in Bucharest without *ciorbă*. I am going to die."

According to Paula, it is very rare that a student does not receive food from home. In Cluj, I met one young man who intended to study in the Netherlands. So what would he do about food? "I will ask my mother to put the food on a plane," he said with a smile.

I am not at all sure that he was joking.

It was difficult to wrench myself away from Romania, but the goal was the Caucasus so I pressed on, taking a night bus to Istanbul.

There are cities that engage the senses so deeply that the visitor doesn't need to *do* anything. You simply dance in your mind to their magic. Istanbul is one such city, though it faces some challenges.

If a visiting Martian said to me, "Earthling, take me to your three finest cities", I know where we would go. To Venice, a sublime Old World city; to New York, with all the gutsy dynamism of the New; and to Istanbul, the supreme hybrid city, standing astride Europe and Asia like a colossus. There is no other city on earth that bridges two continents.

The great cities draw you back. In early May I arrived for my fifth visit to Istanbul and since my last time forty years ago the place has grown immensely.

The experience of riding through the western suburbs on the night bus from Bucharest brought out the country boy in me. The vast urban landscape of high-rise buildings first numbed my mind and then I wanted to scream, "You've got too big!"

According to the Turkish Statistical Institute, the population of Istanbul at the end of 2013 was 14,160,467 and it is projected to reach 16.6 million by 2023. About a third of the population lives on the Asian side, but this is still Europe's largest urban agglomeration.

Later, seeing that the historic core of the city still wove its charm, I regained some sense of calm.

In all three of my chosen cities, there is the powerful presence of water as a defining element in the landscape. A city needs that to achieve true greatness. None of them today is a capital. They don't have to bother with all that national government stuff and can evolve and direct their energies with more freedom.

All offer sensual experience in the fullest sense. What visitors to Istanbul remember years later is the mix of smells —the saffron in the spice market, the roast chestnuts or sweet corn on Istiklal Avenue, the city's great pedestrian thoroughfare. Some visitors, women as well as men, remember decades later watching the sinuous movements of an Istanbul belly dancer. At its best, and it is done well in Istanbul, this is classy entertainment.

The city is noisy, but its noises are varied and seldom grate, at least not on me. There is the mewing of the ubiquitous cats, the muezzin's call to prayer, Turkish music on the radio, falling rain, hooting cars, chattering travellers. This is one of the world's most popular tourist destinations and even at midnight Istiklal Avenue bursts with humanity. As a moneymaking centre Istanbul is so important that it represents more than a quarter of Turkey's gross domestic product.

There is a dark side, of course, as you would expect in a big complex city. On my first evening, out strolling not far from the Bosphorus shore, I became aware of the clump of heavy boots behind me. I turned and saw about fifteen to twenty policemen, some with riot shields and truncheons at the ready, just metres from me and running in my general direction. Within seconds they passed me and went into a park.

I picked up from other people in the street that they were attentive but not frightened. I took my cue from them. Earlier I had seen a small left-wing demonstration in the city's Taksim Square where riot police were present in their dozens. It was a day in the life of Istanbul.

There have been moments in Istanbul's recent past when riot police were truly out in force. In 2013, for example, there were clashes sparked by plans to turn Gezi Park next to Taksim, the central square, into a shopping mall. Disturbances spread to a number of Turkish towns and cities and at least six protesters and one policeman died.

The government scrapped plans for the shopping mall after the protests, but the Istanbul residents I spoke to were not complacent about the future quality of life in their city. A third international airport is under construction, as is the third Bosphorus bridge.

Some fear that these developments will put more strain on a metropolis already groaning with traffic. My guess is that a long struggle lies ahead for those who do not want Istanbul to be sacrificed on the altar of progress.

After a few days in Istanbul, I set out on the long bus ride right across Turkey to Georgia.

CHAPTER 2

First Impressions of Georgia

Church bells. Lying in bed at Batumi on the Black Sea shore, I hear church bells. It is a sound with powerful emotional overtones that sets off memories of home.

After a twenty-one-hour bus ride through Turkey, one of the heartlands of Islam, I am once again in a mainly Christian country. I have arrived in Georgia. It is a little counter-intuitive so far east of Istanbul to be in a land that considers itself so very firmly to be part of Europe and of Christendom.

Georgians and their neighbours to the south, the Armenians, are proud of being the first nations to convert to Christianity early in the fourth century, before Theodosius adopted it as the state church of the Roman Empire in AD 380.

I am staying in a hostel in Batumi's Old Town, an attractive medley of houses, many with balconies. Batumi is known for its variety of architectural styles, including Art Nouveau, Art Deco, Neoclassical and Italian Baroque.

I pop out to a corner shop to buy milk for my breakfast. The shopkeeper has a face that seems to be a landscape of nervous tics. He picks up a bottle of something which is patently not milk and pours me a shot, all the while winking and saying in Russian, "Home-made, home-made". Eventually, despite the earliness of the hour, I feel obliged to down the lot. This is, of course, an attempt at a sale, but it feels like my first encounter with the legendary alcoholic hospitality of Georgia.

Batumi is the first Georgian town I have seen. It is both port and seaside resort, but Batumi has neither golden sands nor crashing surf. A wide pebble beach stretches south as far as the eye can see and the Black Sea with its modest waves looks a little like a giant millpond.

I have never felt quite the same about this stretch of water since reading Neal Ascherson's masterly book *Black Sea*.

Ascherson writes, "The Black Sea is the world's biggest single reservoir of hydrogen sulphide. Below a fluctuating depth of between 150 and 200 metres, there is no life."

The huge accumulation of H_2S has occurred because five major rivers run into the Black Sea – the Danube, Kuban, Don, Dnieper and Dniestr. The great volume of organic matter from these rivers has shaped the composition of the sea. The Mediterranean, by contrast, receives the water of only three major rivers, the Rhône, Nile and Po.

Batumi has sought to supplement what the Almighty has given it with some very attractive gardens and pedestrian boulevards set back slightly from the shore and a series of initiatives which include a gambling industry. A taxi driver tells me that Batumi has fifteen casinos. They certainly loom large in the town and if you itch to bet a fortune at the gaming tables there is no lack of opportunity.

I have hit a seaside resort in the off-season, early May, and it is what it is. One evening I am the only customer dining in a restaurant in the Old Town. Into this very sleepy atmosphere slips a brisk young man who sits at a nearby table. In clear North American tones he tells the waitress, "I am from New York." Then, after a brief pause, he adds, "It is very quiet." There the conversation ends, confirming his point.

Batumi has not always been quiet. Historically, western Georgia has played a very canny game, with involvement in the key commodities of the era. Wealth, at least for an elite, and occasional violence have been running themes.

In the ancient world, this region was one of the centres of gold and silver mining. According to the Georgian National Museum, gold mining began in Georgia in the fourth and third millennia BC. Western Georgia was the ancient kingdom of Colchis, which features in one of the most famous stories in world literature.

This is where Jason came with his Argonauts to steal the Golden Fleece. In Batumi they have erected a very tall monument to Medea, daughter of a king of Colchis who fell in love with Jason and became his wife.

There is still gold in them thar hills, but in the nineteenth and twentieth centuries it was oil that caught the attention of entrepreneurs, revolutionaries and governments.

In 1901 a young Georgian revolutionary later known to the world as Stalin came to Batumi and soon found work with the Rothschilds who owned an oil refinery in the town.

According to British historian Simon Sebag Montefiore, "On Stalin's first day at work the Rothschilds' refinery mysteriously caught fire." Stalin spent some time imprisoned in Batumi.

But this Bolshevik arsonist did not halt the march of the Caucasus oil industry. In 1906 the world's first long-distance oil pipeline opened, linking the oilfields of Baku on the Caspian Sea to Batumi, which was now clearly a nerve centre of the world economy.

A few years later the British came to Batumi, drawn like Stalin not by the charm of the pebble shore but by the oil. A British military officer backed by 20,000 troops briefly ruled the region just after the First World War.

I feel that I have arrived in a country with so many interesting threads that I could sit for years writing, writing and writing.

I had never associated Georgia with the Romans, but the Empire did extend this far and one day I make an outing with a fellow traveller, a young Lithuanian woman, to the ruins of the Roman fortress of Gonio between Batumi and the Turkish border. The walls of the fortress, 900 metres long and five metres high, are remarkably well preserved. By coincidence I had visited Hadrian's Wall in northern England just three months earlier and it is hard to take in how vast that empire was. The visit to Gonio was an early reminder that Georgia is replete with history.

One thread struck me as particularly important when I travelled on to Tbilisi, six hours away by bus, about 360 kilometres. I crossed more than half the country. My overwhelming impression was how green and lush Georgia is, how richly covered with trees.

I dug out a few official statistics. Nearly forty percent of Georgia's territory is forest. England, by contrast, has a little over eight percent of its land covered by forest and even back in the eleventh-century Domesday records show that the figure was only fifteen percent.

Georgia can still boast of brown bears, wolves, lynx and jackals, indeed more indigenous animals than any country in Europe except for Russia.

For the past five weeks I have been either in cities or on buses and trains. I feel the call of the High Caucasus and I must away.

CHAPTER 3

In the Caucasus at Last

Georgia's Mount Kazbek on the border with Russia

I try to rein in the superlatives, but never in all my days have I been anywhere lovelier than the Caucasus in spring.

Being here is an experience that ripples right through me, like opening up to a new love.

I am staying in a village called Lenjeri in Georgia's northwestern region of Svaneti, known beyond its borders for its stunning mountain landscapes, ancient stone towers and living traditions of music and dance.

Let me give some geographical context. The border with Russia is twelve kilometres to the north of Lenjeri. Mount Elbrus, Europe's highest peak, is about forty kilometres to the northwest, inside Russia, and Sochi, the Russian resort which hosted the 2014 Winter Olympics, some 250 kilometres to the west on the Black Sea coast.

When I walk out of my guesthouse, the view westward is sublime –spring flowers, trees in blossom and a mountain range covered in snow.

Several times now I have walked from my guesthouse along the road to Mestia, a town about forty minutes by foot to the east. I feel familiar with the road's sights and sounds. Every day there are men ploughing the rich earth with oxen, a team of two animals for one plough. Pigs usually scavenge by the roadside. Up on the woodland slopes towards Russia I often hear the call of a cuckoo.

I see the Svan stone towers, between twenty and twenty-five metres tall, built over the centuries to protect villagers from attack. These are such a powerful presence in the land, a statement of continuity with a world rooted in the family and the blood feud.

Typically, the top floor is a big room built to accommodate a family and hold stocks to see them through a hard winter or a long siege. Many towers go back to the twelfth and thirteenth centuries and are an important part of what distinguishes Svaneti from practically anywhere else on earth. They are intended to protect families from avalanches or from enemies, who historically could have been the next-door neighbour or an invader. Blood feuds between families passed into history only within the last few years.

The Svans have been around for a very long time and they

have had a fearsome reputation as warriors. The Greek geographer Strabo, born in the first century BC, wrote that the Svans were "foremost in courage and power" and could put in the field an army of 200,000 men. Even today in Svaneti, Georgians quote to the visitor Strabo's praise for this proud people.

The Svans have their own unwritten language, related to but distinct from Georgian.

Before the twentieth century it was difficult to reach Svaneti and the way of life in this remote mountain fastness changed little. The first car arrived in 1935 – indeed the wheel came in the same lifespan as the television. The Svans traditionally used sledges because wheeled carts are useless in the snow.

The region reminds me a little of Transylvania, in the sense that it is another example of a peasant society producing much of its own food and another great feast for the eye.

In case you decide to come to Svaneti, let me tell you how I got here.

Take the centre of Tbilisi, the Georgian capital, as the starting point. From Freedom Square, ride the metro out four stops to Samgori. An announcer tells you in English which stop is coming up next. (This is useful. Bear in mind that Georgian has its own beautiful but daunting alphabet.)

Leaving Samgori station, emerge onto the road and turn right. After about 100 metres there is a small area where a few minibuses are usually parked and a sign in our alphabet says Mestia – the main town in Svaneti.

The fare for the eight-hour journey is 30 lari. (Exchange rates in 2017 were about 2.3 lari to the US dollar, 3.1 to the pound).

The vehicle for the run to Mestia is a Nissan Serena SUV. For the first hour we do the rounds in Tbilisi, picking up passengers. Eventually we set out with Giorgi at the wheel, plus five adults, two children and luggage. As the sole foreigner, I get the seat of honour in the front.

The journey takes us past Gori, Stalin's birthplace, where the Caucasus are already in view. When we stop at a modern roadside store, a few young men emerge from the shop and burst into very melodious song. My goodness, we don't get that at home! This is my first experience of the celebrated tradition of Georgian polyphonic singing.

We continue on to Zugdidi, not very far inland from the Black Sea. To the Anglo-Saxon ear, this name does not sound promising, but Zugdidi turns out to be a fetching town with fountains, gardens and views of the snow-capped ranges to the north.

After Zugdidi we start to climb and soon Giorgi is negotiating a serious mountain road. For lunch we stop at a roadside restaurant in the mountains. Driver and passengers sit at one table. Tasty Georgian fare appears and we all tuck in. Giorgi refuses to let me make any financial contribution to lunch and we press on.

I have a contact in Svaneti, the friend of a friend of an old Reuters pal. His name is Vakhtang Pilpani. Both he and his father are noted musicians in Svaneti and he runs a guesthouse.

Giorgi calls him on his mobile phone and says that we have reached his village, Lenjeri. Giorgi has barely finished the call when we stop in front of a vehicle parked in the road. It is Vakhtang.

With black pigs scampering at our feet – there are always animals on Georgian roads – we transfer my luggage to Vakhtang's vehicle. Almost immediately Vakhtang, a man with a Falstaffian girth and a sense of theatre, delivers a short discourse on the English language.

"There are three kinds of English," he tells me grandly. "There is American English, British English and Svanetian English. I am a specialist in Svanetian English."

I discover that English is actually Vakhtang's fourth language after Svan, Georgian and Russian. When I tell him that I have some Russian he is visibly relieved.

I chill out in Vakhtang's comfortable home, just drinking the place in. I love the names of the mountains – Ushba, Tetnuldi, Shkhara, Akhalgazrdoba, Chkhunderi, Mudurbani. They are such appropriately hard names for mountains made of granite and shale.

When I hear a Svan speak the name of Ushba or Shkhara I feel I am listening to a character out of the pages of Tolkien. Some of that granite has surely entered Svaneti's DNA – these people are tough, severe and unsmiling. They are also skilled musicians, producing deep sonorous sounds that go way back in the human story.

Svan music is known internationally and Vakhtang tells me that his father, eighty-one-year-old Eptime Islam Pilpani, has been to Paris three times to perform as a musician.

I am lucky enough to hear Vakhtang and his music group play for some German tourists. Vakhtang tells me that several of the songs the group is singing date back 4,000 years.

The evening's entertainment includes a virtuoso linguistic performance by the Germans' tour guide, a young Svanetian woman. She translates all of Vakhtang's comments about the music, spoken in the Svan language, into German. As she tells me, "Es ist nicht einfach." Not easy at all, I can imagine, but this tour guide, Tea Totogashvili, surely has one of the world's ultimate niche products.

The future for her mother tongue does not look bright. No one really knows how many Svan speakers there are, but *Ethnic Groups of Europe: an Encyclopedia* says the number is probably no more than 30,000. It says Svan branched off from the Kartvelian languages' common ancestor in the eighteenth century before Christ.

To see more of Svaneti I will be travelling by foot. Mestia is nearly the end of the road for all motorised transport except jeeps.

With Vakhtang's help, I find a Georgian guide to accompany me. Lasha Tkeshelashvili is a young man with good English and solid trekking experience. The aim is to walk for four days, with Ushguli, one of Europe's highest settlements, as our destination.

22 May 2015

We head east out of Mestia and the town's small airport below us looks even tinier as we climb through woodland and meadow. With great mountain views to the north of us, Lasha talks about how local people used to cross these high places to find work in Russia.

"My grandfather has told me that in Soviet times many men from Svaneti used to cross by foot through passes to Russia, to Kabardino-Balkaria. If they started out at five by two or three in the afternoon they could be in a small Russian town called Baksan."

After the dissolution of the Soviet Union and a five-day war between Georgia and Russia in 2008 no one crosses these passes today.

Lasha also talks about how he came to choose guiding.

"When I was nine years old my grandfather took me to a glacier for the first time. He was taking cows and bulls to the fields and we continued to the glacier. A year later I took my younger brother there. For me it was like I took some drug and after that I went to the mountains every summer."

After university he spent three years as a loan expert in a bank, but as he tried to work with loan figures on his computer images of mountains kept dancing before his eyes. So he quit and became a guide.

In a matter of weeks after our walk Lasha is due to marry his fiancée, a young Polish woman from the city of Kraków, and he radiates contentment. He sets the tone for a very cheerful hike.

Shortly we reach the highest point of the day's walk and there are glorious views to the east, looking out over the Mulkhura valley to the snow-capped peak of Tetnuldi beyond. Tetnuldi, at 4,858 metres, is fifty metres higher than Mont Blanc. Lasha tells me that the name means 'eternal snow' in Svan. Then we go down a pine-scented path for a coffee break in the home of a relative.

The rest of the day is an easy walk following the Mulkhura river. Lasha tells me that wolves sometimes swoop down from the forests into this valley and kill livestock, including cows. This tends to happen, he says, at the onset of winter.

Another piece of information is that plans are advanced to build a ski resort. We see the chairs for a lift stacked on the valley floor and pylons for the chair lift are built. Wolves and skiers will soon be sharing a valley. This thought dampens my spirits. I am not thrilled by the constant encroachment of humans into the habitats of other species.

After walking fourteen kilometres we arrive at our guesthouse in the village of Zhabeshi at the top of the valley. The house is distinctively furnished, with a stuffed local bear in the main room and a copy of the tragedies of Shakespeare, in Georgian of course, in my bedroom.

The evening is a real highlight. Before travelling to Georgia I had heard about the tradition of the *supra,* a banquet presided over by a toastmaster called a *tamada.* The guesthouse owner, Giorgi Naveriani, decides that our meal together is a *supra.* He presides and Lasha translates.

We drink home-made apple vodka and Giorgi's first toast is to God. "The first toast is to God everywhere in Georgia," says Lasha. (Later, I hear other opinions on this.)

The second toast is to the archangels Michael and Gabriel – this, says Lasha, is the standard second toast in Svaneti.

The third toast is to St George, which seems only fair. "We believe that St George will give us many sons," explains Lasha.

The fourth toast is to the memory of those who have passed away and we spill a libation on the floor.

Giorgi carries on, "The fifth toast is to peace, first in our souls and in our families and then in the world."

Lasha then proposes the sixth and last toast – to St Mary, who will look after our families.

A little mischievously, I ask Lasha if it would have been acceptable to sneak in a toast to Manchester United, say, as the fifth offering. Lasha is adamant that this would not be acceptable at all. As the sixth toast then? Yes, that would be absolutely fine.

It seems the first five toasts are girded around by strong tradition and all in all I feel I have been given a glimpse of the Georgian sense of the sacred. In my mind I had built up the *tamada* as a rather loud, life and soul of the party type. But Giorgi is softly spoken and this helps to create an atmosphere of fellowship and repose. I find the whole experience profoundly moving.

23 May 2015

We set out in a southerly direction from Zhabeshi and start climbing. After two hours we reach the snow line and walk through groves of rhododendron. We're tackling an ascent of 800 metres, walking up to an altitude of 2,400 metres. Normally this wouldn't be a big deal but snow is a game changer.

"We use twice as much energy in snow," says Lasha and my aching body agrees. We finally reach the highest point of the hike and take a break.

After lunch we're walking along, minding our own business,

when a crackling roar bursts all around us. Then we see smoke rising off the mountain, about 300 metres ahead of us and to the right. Lasha voices my thoughts. "I think that is where the lightning struck."

It is my first experience of thunder and lightning up quite so close and personal. It is utterly terrifying and somehow all of a piece with the grandeur of the Caucasus. Further on we watch an eagle, soaring higher and higher until it is lost from view.

We walk down through great banks of primroses. Suddenly, after an eleven-kilometre walk that has taken seven hours, the village of Adishi comes into view below us. It looks exquisite with its Svan towers.

But when we reach Adishi I revise my view; it looks like a disaster zone. Practically all the stone buildings are in ruins and many of the newer wooden ones are abandoned and in decay. Dotted around in this scene of desolation are a few inhabited houses.

In a sense, Adishi is a disaster zone. Lasha says an avalanche hit it in 1986. No one died, but many buildings were damaged and some villagers left for good. When we reach our guesthouse, the middle-aged owner tells us that eleven families live in Adishi, as opposed to forty-five in his youth.

These remote villages have mains electricity, but today there is a power outage and our dinner is cooked on a wood stove. This does look and feel like back country. Lasha tells me that the nearest school is nine kilometres down a jeep track. The children go off on Monday, stay with family near the school and head home on Friday.

The guesthouse looks after us well; the table is well-laden and the blankets are thick. The peals of laughter that come from the mistress of the household suggest that Adishi has not given up hope.

The village has no fewer than four churches and we visit the tiny medieval church of St George, with frescoes inside and out.

Emotionally, it has been a powerful couple of days. To ground myself in the familiar and to let Lasha hear the sound of Welsh, I play on my phone *Mae Hen Wlad Fy Nhadau*, the Welsh national anthem, as sung by Cerys Matthews.

24 May 2015

From Adishi, the logical route would be through the Chkhutnieri Pass to the southeast, but this 2,722-metre pass is covered in snow and Lasha says that walking there could provoke an avalanche. Instead we walk northwest along the track taken by the schoolchildren, following the tumbling waters of the Adishchala. It is a stroll in the park after the previous day and I see a dipper, bobbing on a stone in the river.

At the village of Bogreshi we join the jeep track to Ushguli which we will follow all the way to our destination. We are alongside the Enguri, another fast-flowing Caucasus river swollen with the melting snows of spring.

Towards the end of the day I suddenly have a 'senior moment' of a type I have never had before. A vehicle passes me, comes to an abrupt halt and a couple of Georgians jump out and head towards me.

A middle-aged woman addresses me and comes straight to the point. "How old are you?" she asks. This is an unusual opening gambit anywhere in the world. I reply truthfully and the woman looks at me open-mouthed. She has her photo taken standing beside this ancient Briton and then returns to her car and goes on her way. It's a unique moment in my travelling career.

After a twenty-two-kilometre walk that takes eight hours, we bed down in a guesthouse in the village of Lalkhori. In the bedroom, a bust of Stalin stares down at us from on top of a wardrobe. It is so much nicer to be greeted by the Bard than by the Vozhd.

25 May 2015

The last leg of the walk to Ushguli. In places this is a very dramatic road – the views to our right are of rocky crags and rushing waters as the Enguri darts through narrow ravines.

One feature of walks in the Caucasus is the need to cross boisterous brooks. Close to Ushguli I cross one on horseback, after a man out cutting firewood lends me his horse.

We cover the nine kilometres to Ushguli in three hours. The village doesn't disappoint – it has atmosphere and history. It is actually a group of four villages, 2,000 to 2,200 metres above sea level, and one of the highest settlements in Europe. Lasha says the medieval Queen Tamar of Georgia had summer and winter residences in Ushguli. The remains of her summer residence stand broodingly on a hill.

Lasha guides me to a homestay, where the lady of the house is providing food and white wine for two elderly neighbours who have spent all day helping her to plant potatoes.

Time for fond farewells from Lasha – it has been such a treat to walk with him. We have hiked together for fifty-six kilometres and our conversations have ranged from the retreat of glaciers to the habits of wolves, from the problems of rural schooling to the Svan hunting goddess Dali.

Back in the late twentieth century, when economic and political turbulence swept the Caucasus, Svaneti acquired an unsavoury reputation for crime. Lasha told me that after the work in Russia dried up, some Svans took to highway robbery to earn a living. But in the early years of this century the Georgian authorities came down hard on bandits. After taking office in 2004, the then president Mikheil Saakashvili dispatched government forces to Svaneti to re-assert Tbilisi's hold over the region. During this trek Svaneti has felt no more dangerous than the English Lake District.

26 May 2015

I do my first solo hiking in the region and set out from Ushguli in glorious sunshine for the glacier on Shkhara, generally considered the highest peak in Georgia and the fourth in Europe. (Its altitude varies depending on which map you consult. The map I am using, by terraQuest, says 5,203 metres. The highest point of Shkhara is in Russia.)

Except for a few wisps of cloud around the summit, Shkhara is visible in all its glory – great ribs of rock but mainly a landscape of snow.

This is one of the classic hikes of Georgia, but I have the trail of eight kilometres practically to myself. The path follows the Enguri river which has its source on Shkhara and it's an easy walk, with the majestic mountain ahead encouraging me on. Towards the end of the hike I see two Georgian border guards and a boy on a horse. I commune mainly with cows and super-abundant frogs.

Nowadays, in the age of climate change, glaciers can induce feelings of melancholy. Work published in 2015 by scientists at the Tbilisi State University said that in 2014 the Shkhara glacier was about 300 metres shorter than in 1960.

I need transport back to Mestia, forty-six kilometres to the northwest and connected mainly by rough jeep track. The going rate for jeep transport is 200 lari (about $87) but I get lucky and hitch a ride with Israeli tourists. They are travelling in a convoy of five SUVs and I am directed into a vehicle of Russian speakers.

Inside the vehicle I am in a different world. A walkie-talkie crackles and conversations on this and on mobile phones set the tone. Suddenly Georgia feels very far away. I learn that my fellow passenger in the back was born in the Ukrainian city of Odessa. He comments that Georgia is poor. With limited Russian I can't respond adequately, but I try to tell him that in all five of the Svanetian houses where I have stayed the families have the usual range of modern things – television, fridge, freezer and washing machine. Lasha tells me that standards of living in the region have risen considerably over the past decade, largely thanks to tourism.

On my return to Mestia, I find that Vakhtang is indisposed. I am told that he was *tamada* at a family *supra* for a deceased aunt. Afterwards he felt rather the worse for wear and the doctor was summoned. While I am still in Mestia he recovers, but the incident is a reminder that the role of *tamada* does carry health risks.

I have enjoyed Svaneti. At the same time I have found that the Svans have an undoubted seriousness about them, a heaviness in truth. Even at the Mestia tourist information office the two women working there seldom smile. Still, you can't have everything. Part of Georgia's charm is precisely that it has not swallowed the ideals of a consumer society hook, line and sinker.

There is one cruel irony about Svaneti. The Svans are doing the right thing by the earth; they plough with bulls for heaven's sake. You can't get more low-carbon than that. During eleven days in Svaneti I saw innumerable bulls at work and just two tractors. But all over the Caucasus the glaciers are melting – scientists tell us that this is because most of the world has rushed into fossil fuels and warmed the planet.

The Svans farm the way that they do not because they have read learned papers on climate change, but because this is the way they have always farmed. I can't shake off the feeling that plough-ing with bulls or horses is the right thing to do. I think of the families ploughing with livestock as heroes of our time.

Aesthetically, the plough has power. The English poet Edward Thomas once wrote: "The ship, the chariot, the plough, these three are, I suppose, the most sovereign beautiful things which man has made in his time, and such that were his race to pass away from the earth, would bring him most worship among his successors."

He added: "And the greatest of all is the plough. It is without pride and also without vanity."

Lands that have forgotten the plough are diminished. Long may it flourish in Svaneti.

This was my first foray into the Greater Caucasus and happily not my last. After Svaneti I head back to Tbilisi and take to the road again, up the grandly named Georgian Military Highway. This two-lane road of uneven quality goes through spectacular country and eventually reaches Russia. The highway goes past the turquoise waters of the Zhinvali Reservoir and the exquisite centuries-old fortress complex of Ananuri by the water's edge.

Then it follows the lush green valley of the river Aragvi until it becomes an extraordinary climb, with hairpin bends galore and almost sheer drops to the valley floor.

North of Gudauri, Georgia's premier ski resort, the road goes over the Jvari (Cross) Pass at 2,379 metres. Cars and trucks share the highway with the occasional large herd of sheep and goats, accompanied by shepherds, dogs and donkeys.

The three-hour ride from Tbilisi to the town of Stepantsminda, close to the Russian border, costs 10 lari ($4.50) or the price of a large latte in a British coffee shop.

Stepantsminda was until recently called Kazbegi and that is still what most people call it. Kazbegi and its surroundings surpass my expectations. To the east is a great wall of peaks, some of which seem in my imagination to have been crafted by a celestial artist out of charcoal and then very lightly sprinkled with snow from a play box.

To the west is one of the famous sights of the Caucasus. There are some places that the camera loves and where a sense of the sacred hangs in the air. In Georgia, there is one church and one mountain where the cameras have surely clicked more than anywhere else.

The fourteenth-century Tsminda Sameba church stands serenely on a hill and to its right soars the redoubtable peak that is Kazbek. There is something about the combination of delicate church and massive peak, of yin and yang, which beguiles my senses. It is such a satisfying sight.

Once upon a time this view was nearly ruined. In 1988 the Soviet authorities completed work on a cable car with a base station in Kazbegi and the top station not very far from the church. Local people felt that it violated the sanctity of the place and they destroyed it. British author Peter Nasmyth tells the story of this spirited act in his book *Georgia: In the Mountains of Poetry*. The abandoned base station is still clearly visible behind the Stepantsminda Historical Museum.

Mount Kazbek's greatest claim to fame is that, according to ancient Greek myth, it was on this peak that Zeus chained the Titan Prometheus for stealing fire from the gods. A raven was sent every day to tear out his liver. How many mountains have a backstory to match that one?

Kazbek, 5,047 metres high, was first scaled by Douglas Freshfield, A.W. Moore and C. Tucker of London's Alpine Club, together with their guide François Devouassoud, in 1868. Freshfield, aged twenty-three at the time, went on to become one of the most distinguished mountaineers of his generation, with a great knowledge of the high places of the Caucasus. He was a reflective man and in one of his books he avers that man will one day conquer the highest peaks of the Himalaya. The use of oxygen bags, he suggests, will be key.

In the final third of the nineteenth century, the British generally were much to the fore in conquering the Caucasus peaks. They often travelled with a volume of Shakespeare or Dickens in their luggage. One common ritual when climbing a previously unscaled mountain was to write their names on a card and leave this in a sardine box in a hastily built cairn.

I have no great ambitions and no sardine box, but I hatch a plan to go at least part way up Kazbek, and hire waterproof boots from a local mountain guiding agency. A man at the agency says that in seven hours at the most I should reach the Bethlemi mountain hut on the far side of a glacier called Gergeti.

I make that my goal and with sleeping bag and food in my rucksack I set out shortly after 10am in light rain, knowing that the weather forecast is for thunderstorms.

But after half an hour the sun comes out and the walk up to the church is a pleasant stroll on a dirt road, first through the village of Gergeti and then through a pine woodland full of birdsong.

At the stone church and bell tower on the hill I stop to pay my respects to this triumph of human determination and then push on up a ridge. I reach the first snow and finally, after nearly six hours on the hoof, I stand by the cross on the Arsha Pass, altitude 2,940 metres.

From here there is a good panoramic view of the Gergeti glacier and Mount Kazbek. This is the limit for day-trippers and now the path gets lonelier, through a wild landscape of rock, snow and ice. I can see why Zeus would have thought this a good place to punish Prometheus.

At 6:55pm, after cresting a rise in the snow on the glacier, I see the mountain hut for the first time, perched on a little plateau on the other side. Aesthetically, the Bethlemi hut is not as pleasing as the church, but emotionally it holds out the promise of safety and warmth.

I am now at 3,250 metres and have symptoms of altitude sickness – shortage of breath, light-headedness and nausea. This is normal and I go slowly, stopping every few paces to rest.

The trodden path across the glacier is easy to follow and there are no dizzying crevasses. This is a plod across a snowfield. After forty minutes or so I leave the Gergeti glacier behind and begin the final climb to the hut.

This is the toughest part of the whole walk, a scramble over rocks and snow with no discernible path. My energy is fading and so is the light. Finally, at 8:20 in the evening, after more than ten hours' walking, I reach the hut, which at first sight seems empty. It is a big place, built to accommodate 200 people. But at the far end of the hut there is a small knot of men outside and an open door. I am led into a cluttered Dickensian kitchen.

In the best traditions of Georgian hospitality a mug of piping hot tea is placed before me within minutes of my arrival. Bliss beyond compare! I savour every last mouthful and ask for more.

For a fellow old enough to get a British state pension, I haven't done too badly. Today's ascent of about 1,930 metres, much of it in snow, is the equivalent of going from sea level to the top of Snowdon, Wales's highest peak, about 1.75 times. I will remember this day.

At 3,670 metres one moves in elevated circles. I am suddenly in the company of mountaineers. In such places there is an instant spark of solidarity. We are snug and warm inside, drinking tea, and the cold of the Caucasus night is without. What more do you need for a bit of bonding? "We few, we happy few, we band of brothers…"

I chat to a Muscovite and to another Russian from the Siberian city of Krasnoyarsk. My mental faculties are not at their sharpest. What I understand is that they are part of a six-person team, which includes a New Zealander, and they're set on climbing Mount Kazbek, which is smack on the border with Russia. To bed, exhausted.

In the morning there is great excitement. We hear the clatter of a helicopter and rush out to discover what is happening. It turns out to be the changing of the guard at the Bethlemi hut. The outgoing team has clambered into a helicopter, which has landed close by, and out come two men with new energy and fresh Georgian bread. They have arrived for a ten-day stint.

The helicopter stays only a couple of minutes, takes off, turns, flies low over the glacier and heads for home.

The walk back to Kazbegi is uneventful. The next day I go into a restaurant and there is the man from Krasnoyarsk sitting with a fellow climber. They call me over and we chat. I discover that in my addled state two days earlier I had misunderstood them. When we met they were actually on their way down after scaling Kazbek.

Ah! So, how was it? "Oozhasno," says the man from Krasnoyarsk and I can't help reflecting on what a perfect word the Russians have for "terrible". He describes walking in the bitter cold, in snow that was up to his thighs.

After a few moments he takes his leave and walks towards the door with a very pronounced limp. He glances back at me with one final look that says, "I told you it was tough."

CHAPTER 4

June Days in Georgia

It is a little early in the year still for the mountain passes of the Caucasus, but I decide to travel southeast along the Sno valley to the little village of Juta. My idea is to walk east from there, over a high pass, to the region called Khevsureti. I do the journey of about twenty kilometres to Juta by taxi – it is too remote for *marshrutky*, the shared minibuses serving as public transport on fixed routes in the former Soviet Union – and check in to a homestay run by Soso Arabuli.

I arrive in Juta on 6 June. Soso, in his mid-fifties, is a friendly, informative soul and he tells me that the trail to Khevsureti, going over the 3,338-metre Chaukhi Pass, is still snow-bound. So that idea bites the dust.

Juta feels like the coolest inhabited place I have ever been during a northern hemisphere June. There is a real chill, a dampness in the air and not a lot of sun.

It is a tough life in this Caucasus village, with snow carpeting the landscape for much of the year and temperatures dropping in winter to -23C. Not surprisingly, Juta has been shrinking for decades. Soso says that in his youth about thirty-seven families lived here. Today the number has dropped down to sixteen or seventeen in the summer and ten in the winter. "The road is closed from November and re-opens the end of April, beginning of May," says Soso.

He shows me an old photo, dating back to 1955, of a class of children from the village school which closed about eight years ago. It is a poignant image – closure of a school tears the heart out of a place. Where does it go from there?

During one of our conversations, a younger male relative of Soso's joins us for a while and I get the usual "Where are you from?" question. My answer leads him to whip out his mobile phone and here in the Greater Caucasus he slowly conjures up a map of Wales. The Internet came too late to save the school at Juta, but surely it now carries the potential to be a game changer for small communities everywhere.

Although the Chaukhi Pass is closed, there is still some great walking hereabouts and the next morning I set out in a south-easterly direction towards Mount Chaukhi. I pass a tourist camp called Zeta with an information board describing Juta, altitude about 2,300 metres, as the second highest permanently inhabited place in Europe.

Chaukhi is a splendid series of volcanic rock peaks nicknamed the Dolomites of Georgia. In sunny weather I walk up to the snow line, but don't attempt any fancy mountaineering. This is another beautiful wild landscape of snow, ice and rock and occasionally I pass great slabs of stone.

Returning back down to Juta I sometimes have difficulty in making my way across mountain streams. Again and again in the Caucasus walkers have to gauge where they can safely leap across the water and where the distance is simply too great. I get back without mishap.

The next day I just walk out of Juta after breakfast, back the way I came along the dirt road heading to the Georgian Military

Highway. After a couple of hours hiking, with views of Mount Kazbek ahead of me, I pick up a lift back to Kazbegi.

It feels about time for a change of scene. Off and on I have been in the mountains now for about three weeks. After one night in Kazbegi I take a *marshrutka* back down to Tbilisi – time to savour the lowlands a little.

Just outside Tbilisi is the old Georgian capital, Mtskheta. This will be my next outing. It's a real Georgian tongue twister of a name. On YouTube there is a short clip devoted to pronunciation of this word – it comes out something like Mut Scared Er.

Tbilisi is pretty good at doing the big-city thing of belching cars and rushing traffic, but Mtskheta, just twenty kilometres to the northwest, is an oasis of calm. It is an affluent, ancient town with a walled medieval cathedral at its core. I arrive to find cherries hanging on the trees and wedding parties threading their way through the centre. This is a popular place in Georgia for couples to tie the knot.

The great glory of Mtskheta is the Svetitskhoveli Cathedral, built in the early eleventh century, and one of the holiest places in Georgia. Rather incongruously, the cathedral is surrounded by an eighteenth- century wall with gun emplacements. The building has survived various challenges, from an earthquake in 1283 to Mongol invasion. The first church on this site goes back to the fourth century. In 337 AD, when Georgia adopted Christianity as its official religion, St Nino advised King Mirian to build a church here, over a grave where Christ's robe was said to be buried. According to tradition, a Mtskheta Jew was in Jerusalem at the time of the Crucifixion and he returned home with the robe, which he had bought from a Roman soldier at Golgotha.

I decide to have a guide and hire Darina Megrelishvili, who offers me a tour in Russian or French. I opt for French. I had read in Ryszard Kapuściński's book *Imperium* two memorable stories about this cathedral. First, that the Russians in the nineteenth century whitewashed over priceless frescoes, destroying them forever. Second, that the ruler of the day in the eleventh century had ordered that the architect, Arsukidze, lose a hand so that he never again worked on a project of such magnificence.

Darina speaks with deep indignation about the Russian destruction of the frescoes, carried out in the 1830s ahead of a planned visit by Tsar Nicholas I. "They wanted to clean out the history and the culture of a very ancient country," says Darina, adding, "The Muslims took out the eyes (from frescoes), but only the Russians whitewashed them." In the end, the tsar never even visited Mtskheta, then in an outlying part of his empire. It is clear that the destruction still rankles in the town. The local tourist office mentions the vandalism in its leaflet on the cathedral, adding that other unspecified premises were blown up to "settle down" the territory.

So what about the story of the poor architect? Darina is adamant that there is no truth to this legend, which once appeared in a novel. I believe her and am heartily glad.

There is another very holy place hereabouts and that is Jvari Church atop a nearby rocky outcrop above the muddy confluence of the Mtkvari and Aragvi rivers. The church marks the spot where King Mirian put up a wooden cross after St Nino converted him to Christianity. It was built in the late sixth and early seventh century. I walk there from Mtskheta, over a footbridge and a busy highway and onto the hill. I get a little lost, but while walking through undergrowth I chance upon a tortoise out for its morning constitutional. Jvari Church was for centuries a popular destination for pilgrims and it is still a busy spot today. The church has a simple interior, but you can feel the spiritual imprint of centuries of pilgrimages. The views over Mtskheta and the rivers below are magnificent and I feel the people of Tbilisi are blessed to have all this history, all this beauty, practically on their doorstep.

I walk back down a different way, on a well-trodden path, and am hailed by a young woman in a headscarf who calls me back. Her name is Teona and she wants me to sample the holy water from a spring just below the path. I join her and a few others, who have apparently never met before, and we sit down to a mini *supra* of bread, aubergine, cheese, cucumber and white wine. How easy it is in Georgia to fall into congenial company.

We're in a little grove, with dappled light falling onto paving stones.

People arrive from above and from below carrying plastic containers to stock up on holy water. As we eat, Teona explains about Georgian toasting and I hear from her, as I heard from my guide Lasha in Svaneti, that the first toast is to God. She wants to know how toasting is done in my country. I make a full confession that where I come from we don't have this highly developed culture of toasting. Teona, a devout woman, looks puzzled and I get a slight sense of being a barbarian at a gathering of the enlightened. Soon after, she bids us farewell.

One of the men at the table, Zviad, tells me that his brother has gone fishing and has caught some fish. So we sit down to a second repast.

I don't quite believe this, but here I am on the holiest hill of Christian Georgia eating loaves and fishes.

On the afternoon of 13 June I return to Tbilisi by *marshrutka* and by evening, although I have eaten well, feel ready for a light supper. From my hostel near Freedom Square, my usual habit is to walk down to the Old Town. It takes about ten minutes. But rain is bucketing down and I decide on this occasion just to head into a restaurant immediately opposite the hostel. By the time I leave the place, simply crossing the road back to the hostel is almost like traversing a babbling Caucasus brook. There is such a torrent of brown water tumbling down Leonidze Street that I pay very close attention to where I put my feet.

The next morning the news is dreadful. Flash floods have hit parts of the city – it is Tbilisi's worst disaster in years. Eventually the media report at least twenty human victims. But because the storms devastated the zoo, enabling big cats, bears and wolves to escape, the international media focus largely on Tbilisi as urban jungle. It all becomes a surreal picture story – international TV channels and newspapers show images of a hippopotamus looking rather lost on a Tbilisi street, bears in floodwaters scrambling to survive. An enterprising penguin wins momentary fame because it swims all the way to the Azerbaijan border some sixty kilometres away. At the hostel, we all urge one another to be careful and to watch out for wild cats. Then one day an escaped white tiger in Tbilisi kills a man. It is a very strange few days.

On 14 June there is an impressive turnout in Tbilisi. Thousands of people, many armed with shovels, take part in clean-up operations. Amid the tragedy it is a moving sight, a city pulling together.

CHAPTER 5

Georgia's Most Famous Son, Alas

If Stalin could return to his hometown in the central plains of Georgia, he would have reason to be gratified. More than six decades after his death the modest house where he was born is carefully maintained as a shrine in his honour.

The brick and wood house, now encased within a pavilion, is part of a large museum dedicated to his memory. It pulls in the punters and puts a favourable gloss on the life of one of history's bloodiest mass murderers. To visit the Joseph Stalin museum in Gori is to witness firsthand the human ability to present a selective truth which is a travesty of reality.

Having decided to take the pulse of the Caucasus I cannot ignore this monument to Stalin, born Joseph Vissarionovich Djugashvili. He was by any measure a political colossus of the twentieth century and some Georgians still honour him. The violence of his rule is given very little prominence in Gori.

The first thing you notice about the museum is its sheer size. It is housed in a big palazzo with a tower and a series of arches at ground level, conveying the message that this is a place of substance. Inside, there are carpeted staircases and chandeliers.

Inside the museum they sell Stalin memorabilia, including mugs, watches, pens, pipes, plates, knives, key rings, badges and hip flasks.

Statue of Stalin outside the Gori museum

The great dictator even pops up on market stalls

During my visit an English-speaking guide materialised. A large woman of mature years, she looked as if she had come straight from Soviet central casting. She carried a short stick to point out objects of interest and, presumably, to emphasise her authority.

What followed was an interesting exercise in finely tuned propaganda. The whole performance was skilful to a degree.

She told us things that were interesting and true – always a sound policy. She related that Stalin was a poet who had verse published in the Georgian language, that he was a most gifted singer. An example of Stalin's poetry hangs on a museum wall.

But one rather awkward exhibit she ignored completely. She had nothing to say about a famous postscript written by Lenin in 1923, a year before his death, describing Stalin as "too rough" and calling for his dismissal as general secretary of the Communist Party. Lenin's advice was not heeded.

The museum's treatment of this testament is symbolic of what feels like an ambivalence over how to deal with the whole subject of Stalin. On the one hand, it is to the museum's credit that Lenin's criticism is on display. On the other hand, the text is presented solely in Russian, which limits its usefulness as an exhibit.

The museum has one section on Stalin's family, a delicate topic. The guide told us in neutral tones that Stalin's first wife died of typhus and the second committed suicide. That's the wives dealt with then.

She put the spotlight firmly on his son Yakov, who was a prisoner of war of the Germans in the Second World War. The Germans offered to swap Yakov for Field Marshal Friedrich von Paulus, captured by Soviet forces after the Battle of Stalingrad. But Stalin refused, saying of Soviet soldiers, "All of them are my sons". Yakov died at the Sachsenhausen concentration camp in 1943. The point of the story is clear – Stalin was a leader who wasn't swayed by personal feelings.

It could be argued that a museum dealing with a political leader does not need to focus much on the man's wives. But for the record, Stalin's first wife, Ekaterina (née Svanidze), died at the age of twenty-two after he took her to live in the hot, dirty city of Baku, while he led what British historian Simon Sebag Montefiore called "a life of banditry, espionage, extortion and agitation".

His second wife, Nadya Alliluyeva, shot herself through the heart with a Mauser pistol at the age of thirty-one, after a public row with her husband, by now Soviet leader, at a Kremlin dinner party. She killed herself on 8 November 1932, the day after the fifteenth anniversary of the Bolshevik Revolution. The official announcement said that she died of appendicitis.

Against the odds, the museum creates an upbeat mood, with use of classic Soviet propaganda. There on one wall is an iconic poster of an attractive woman tractor driver, beaming ecstatically as she lives the Soviet dream.

Our guide dealt with the whole subject of the collectivisation of farming in a few brisk sentences and said that "mistakes were made". I saw nothing in the museum about the famines that swept much of the Soviet Union as a result of Stalin's policies.

Welsh journalist Gareth Jones did more than anyone else to alert the world to famine in Ukraine in 1933. Defying a travel ban, he went to Ukraine to see for himself and reported that he found "famine on a colossal scale".

No one knows how many died. The Soviet census of 1937 found eight million people fewer than anticipated. US historian Timothy Snyder, in his book *Bloodlands: Europe between Hitler and Stalin,* wrote of the census, "Stalin suppressed its findings and had the responsible demographers executed."

Snyder estimates that about 3.3 million people died of starvation or hunger-related illness in Soviet Ukraine alone in 1932-1933.

Another subject ignored in the Gori museum is Stalin's treatment of the citizens of other countries.

Many Polish tourists come to Georgia, but I can't imagine that the museum in Gori is high on their list of priorities. One of Stalin's crimes that will live in infamy is the Katyn Forest massacre of about 22,000 Poles in 1940. Stalin's government blamed the Nazis, but the Moscow government finally admitted in 1990 that it was Soviet bullets that ended so many Polish lives.

It is hard to read about these killings even today without shedding a tear. The victims were mainly Polish officers but also included engineers, doctors, lawyers, teachers, priests and journalists. They had fallen into Soviet hands after the Soviet Union invaded Poland in 1939 and the motivation for the slaughter seems to have been to weaken any future Polish state.

The chief executioner of the Soviet NKVD secret police, Vasily Blokhin, carried out many of the killings. Wearing a butcher's leather apron and cap, he personally shot 7,000 Poles over twenty-eight nights.

The only part of the museum devoted to the subject of Stalinist violence is two small rooms on the ground floor, a section added in 2010. One room is a reconstructed secret police interrogation room and the other is a prison cell and antechamber displaying some of the clothes of Gori citizens arrested and shot under Stalin.

Our guided tour of the museum ended in a railway carriage which Stalin used for the last twelve years of his life – he didn't like flying. Standing in the carriage's dining room, I asked our guide what Gori citizens feel about Stalin today.

"I don't know," she said, and then after a slight pause added, "I think most of the older generation like Stalin." Any other answer would have stretched credibility. The guide's entire commentary throughout the tour had a tone of deep respect and admiration.

Back in Tbilisi after my Gori visit, strap-hanging in the city's metro, I noticed that a man next to me was reading a magazine article which included a photo of Stalin looking every inch the handsome father of the nation. Monster though he was, Stalin is clearly a part of the mental landscape of Georgia still.

British writer Peter Nasmyth recounts that in Svaneti, which in 1942 was just one mountain range away from the furthest thrust of Nazi troops, nearly half a century later a Georgian proposed a toast "To Stalin our great general". Nasmyth writes that he raised his glass with everyone else.

CHAPTER 6

Living on the Edge – Vardzia and David Gareji

View of the medieval cave city of Vardzia

The cave-city of Vardzia in southern Georgia is surely one of the wonders of the medieval world, a burst of imperial exuberance.

Georgians built this extraordinary place, conceived as both monastery and citadel, in the twelfth and thirteenth centuries, at the height of their country's power.

An immense network of tunnels, residences, churches, barns,

wine cellars, stables and libraries were hewn from the living rock. The Persian chronicler Hasan Bey Rumlu described Vardzia as a wonder, "impregnable as the wall of Alexander the Great".

A four-hour journey by *marshrutka* took me from Tbilisi first to the leafy town of Borjomi, famous for its mineral water, and then on to Akhaltsikhe, a pretty place dominated by a medieval castle. The road followed the upper reaches of the Mtkvari, the river on which Tbilisi stands.

The surrounding hills on the approach to Vardzia are rocky and arid, but the valley is green and alluring, popular with picnickers. This entire region, called Samtse-Javakheti, is dotted with fortresses and churches. But the jewel in the crown is Vardzia, not far from the Turkish border.

A couple of kilometres from the ruined city I found myself a farm bed and breakfast, next door to a nunnery. It was the rural idyll, Georgia style – a few cows, some hens, thirteen beehives, apple trees, walnuts, maize and sunflowers. As I breakfasted outdoors, a brood of chicks headed off with mum in the direction of the walnut grove.

The Vardzia site, close to the fast-flowing Mtkvari river, opened at 10am and I was there on the dot. In the heat of a Georgian July you don't want to scramble over a rock face under the midday sun. The caves stretch along the cliff for about 500 metres, up to thirteen tiers deep.

Even today, with the help of handrails and wooden steps, it benefits the visitor if she has a few wild-goat genes in her DNA. Some of the time I found myself shinning up or down tunnels and then emerging to admire the view from a totally different vantage point.

Vardzia was designed to be self-sufficient in the event of siege, and that meant a lot of work. According to my audio guide, a tunnel five kilometres long was cut into the cliff wall, about seven metres above the ground, to convey water from springs.

The tunnel had enough headroom for residents to check that there were no problems with the ceramic piping. The water supply could provide up to 207,360 litres per day, enough for up to 3,600 people.

The construction of this mind-boggling structure coincided with a period of expansion and self-confidence, Georgia's Golden Age.

Building began during the reign of Giorgi III (1156-1184), who clearly graduated from the School for Strong Medieval Kingship. Giorgi faced a rebellion by nobles who wanted to put his nephew on the throne. He suppressed the revolt and ordered his nephew to be blinded and castrated.

Work at Vardzia continued during the reign of Giorgi's daughter Queen Tamar (1184-1213), the most revered monarch in the country's history. The Georgian Orthodox Church has made her a saint. During her reign Georgia grew to the peak of its power, holding sway over lands from modern-day eastern Turkey, through the South Caucasus and into western Persia.

Vardzia became a spiritual, economic and political centre, with 420 storerooms and wine cellars and fifteen churches. A chronicler describes how Queen Tamar addressed her troops from the balcony of Vardzia's main place of worship, the church of Holy Dormition, before the battle of Basian against the Seljuk Turks. This battle, fought around 1203 in what is now northeast Turkey, was a victory for the Georgians.

The Dormition church contains a famous wall painting of Queen Tamar, an iconic piece of medieval Georgian art.

In 1283, an earthquake seriously damaged Vardzia as a citadel. But it lived on until Persian troops captured it in 1551, after fighting in the tunnels themselves.

Today five monks live at Vardzia, sharing the cliff with thousands of birds such as martins and swifts who help to bestow on this exquisite place a sense of peaceful sanctuary.

I also visited another rock-hewn monastic complex on the edge of the Christian world, David Gareji, in the southeast of the country on the border with Azerbaijan. It was founded in the sixth century by David Gareji, one of thirteen Assyrian holy men who arrived to spread Christianity.

Like Vardzia, David Gareji is an enchanting place with exuberant wildlife, including Egyptian vultures. The day I arrived it was alive with flowers, lizards and dancing butterflies. The guidebooks say to be careful of poisonous vipers, but I didn't spot any.

Again like Vardzia, David Gareji's heyday was during the Golden Age of Georgia and it grew into an important religious and cultural centre with hundreds of caves, serving as monastic cells, churches and refectories.

David Gareji was the scene of a terrible massacre in 1615, when on Easter night Persian soldiers led by Shah Abbas killed 6,000 monks and destroyed artistic treasures. The monasteries never fully recovered. They closed after the Bolshevik conquest of Georgia in 1921.

In the late twentieth century the Soviet Union used David Gareji as a firing range, training its forces as it fought a war in Afghanistan. Georgian protests against this Soviet desecration of a holy site were part of a swelling nationalist movement which led to Georgia's recovery of independence in 1991.

When the Georgian army returned to the bad old ways of Soviet times in the late 1990s, activists camped out on the site and put a stop to the military exercises.

Four hundred years after the massacre of the monks, this region still feels quite empty of human beings. The landscape is lunar, green in the early summer but still with a feeling of the desert.

Today at David Gareji monastic life has revived in a minor key – there is one working monastery, Lavra, with ten monks. This picture-postcard monastery has both solar panels and monastic cells cut from the rock.

From Lavra, I walked up onto the ridge and took in the great sweeping views of the Azerbaijani plains below. A footpath leads down on the other side to the caves of the Udabno monastery, with frescoes from the Middle Ages.

There is a low-level border dispute between Georgia and Azerbaijan over the David Gareji site. Ideally, Georgia would like the monasteries on the Azerbaijan side to be brought back into its national territory.

Walking along the narrow path to regain the ridge after visiting the caves I nearly bumped into two well-armed Azerbaijan border guards. We exchanged warm greetings and I walked on back into Georgia.

CHAPTER 7

Tbilisi Mon Amour

A part of me doesn't really want to spread the word about Tbilisi at all. This place is the way the world's capital cities used to be before mass tourism – and I love it.

From the tourist's point of view, the Georgian capital comes close to perfection. It's beautiful, cheap and offers stimulating conversation. The streets are safe from crime and the food is exquisite. What more could one possibly ask?

If one were determined to gripe, then the heat of the high summer could be counted against it. As I write on a sweltering August day, BBC Weather says the maximum temperature will be 39C – the same as Khartoum, which stands out in my memory as one very hot city.

(Tbilisi owes its name to an Old Georgian word meaning 'warm location', but that is a reference to the city's many hot springs rather than its climate.)

The first thing that struck me when I saw Tbilisi was the dramatic topography, the cliff rising up sheer on the northern side of the Mtkvari river with a church and other buildings perched on top. I find this view thrilling every time I come back to the city.

The other thing was the charm of the main boulevard, Rustaveli Avenue, with its plane trees soaring to the heavens, the well-dressed women and the lovely balconies of the houses, a feature in much of Tbilisi. So, this is a city that marries drama and elegance.

The topographical extravagance does not end with the cliff. If you wander past Tbilisi's sulphur baths on the south side of the river, you soon come to a canyon and a waterfall. A serious waterfall in the middle of a national capital!

Then the land rises steeply to the Solalaki ridge on the southern side of the city, with the Mother Georgia (Kartvlis Deda) statue and the ancient Narikala fortress. On the other side of the ridge stretches the green expanse of the National Botanical Garden of Georgia, all 161 hectares of it.

It is true that many Tbilisi streets are somewhat dilapidated, but I never found that a turn-off. Smack in the heart of Tbilisi are slightly run-down residential streets. I have no idea how much longer these streets will survive, but I like the fact that people actually live in the very centre of Tbilisi. It is not all banks and bistros.

Scattered here and there are examples of ultra-modern architecture. Much of this, to my mind, does not blend with the rest of Tbilisi. The buildings seem to be there as a political statement, to polish Georgia's credentials as a part of modern Europe.

But it's clear that in human terms Tbilisi is not a carbon copy of the West. While church attendance in Western Europe has been falling, Tbilisi's churches are full to bursting. On a visit to the city's Sioni cathedral I find it packed with worshippers of all generations. The canny ones are outside seated on benches in the courtyard – more comfortable than standing inside.

Tbilisi feels like the main meeting place in the South Caucasus. Here you can rub shoulders with a great variety of people and learn new things. I like to call it the University of the Road – the knowledge one gains from others when on the move. Tbilisi has a lively branch of this august institution.

The backstreets of Tbilisi with Mother Georgia standing tall

One of my teachers in Tbilisi is Yuri Millarson. The first time I met him in a hostel I just learned the basics – he is from San Francisco and he's named after Soviet cosmonaut Yuri Gagarin, the first man in space. In later conversations I realised that Yuri lives, breathes, eats and sleeps the Caucasus like no one else I have ever met. His knowledge is extraordinary and his ideas on day trips unconventional.

One evening he told me that the next day he hoped to go to the Pankisi Gorge in eastern Georgia to brush up on his Chechen grammar with the Kists. The trip didn't happen, in fact, but the conversation improved my knowledge of the ethnic mosaic of Georgia. The Kists trace their origins to the Chechens of the North Caucasus.

Yuri, aged forty-three when I met him, hangs out some of the time with Georgian bikers. He describes himself as an anarchist and he has one very big idea. He wants to foster a sense of the cultural unity of the Caucasus, north and south, so that eventually the peoples of the region can move towards some kind of political union.

So how did a Californian come to be passionate about the Caucasus?

"Well, when I was a child I saw Werner Herzog's *Nosferatu*," said Yuri. "It had *Tsintskaro* playing in it, a very old Georgian vocal polyphonic song and that was my first introduction to the music of the Caucasus actually. As I was growing up as a child the Caucasus was this kind of strange, mythical place."

"And then there was this thing about my grandmother," added Yuri, "my grandmother who was living on the Black Sea coast when she was a little child with her mother." He said the draw of the Caucasus was like going back into an ancestral past, like 'a 1,000-year-old smell'.

Yuri said that for more than twenty years he had been thinking about the unification of the Caucasus, about breaking down what he called "the manufactured distance" between people on different sides of political borders.

"Georgians know very little about Chechens, for example, even though they are direct border neighbours," said Yuri. Since the breakup of the Soviet Union, Chechens have fought two independence wars against Russia but are still part of the Russian Federation.

How could an outsider from California, I asked, bring change to the Caucasus? His answer came swiftly. "You need some different thinking, some outside thinking."

Immediately after my first conversation with Yuri about Caucasus unity, I met two delightful young Russians from the North Caucasus, a brother and a sister in their twenties. He was a lawyer, she was a teacher of English.

Our paths crossed briefly in a restaurant and we arranged to meet the next day. They were Russian citizens of ethnic Armenian stock, visiting family in the Georgian capital. They seemed almost to be embodying Yuri's idea of Caucasus unity.

We ate ice cream and chatted for hours about life, the universe and everything. Sometimes you hear the view in the West that Russians are brainwashed by their media into believing what their government wants them to believe.

The brother and sister, however, told me that they had completely stopped watching Russian television. Her favourite viewing was *Downton Abbey*, not generally regarded as Kremlin propaganda.

Memories of a few excursions and hangouts in Tbilisi will stay with me. One weekend Yuri and I set out to visit the ruins of a Zoroastrian fire temple. Our taxi driver repeatedly got lost and eventually dropped us somewhere close. We asked several Georgians for directions but just got blank looks. Eventually a foreign tourist showed us the way.

Perhaps it was the summer heat, but it then took us half an hour to get in. We finally knocked on the right door and a man opened up what looked like a private home. He pointed languidly to the temple entrance and disappeared.

The temple, called the Ateshgah, is a cuboid brick structure in the south of the city below the Mother Georgia statue and just to the east of the Zemo Betlemi church. It is without windows and essentially featureless. A sign outside says it was probably built between the fifth and seventh centuries, when Zoroastrianism was spreading in Georgia.

The point in going was not to savour architectural greatness, but to get a sense of contact with a very distant past. Zoroaster, the religion's founder, lived in the first or second millennium BC in ancient Iran and developed a monotheistic religion with concepts of heaven and hell. The religion still exists, mainly in India.

In an utterly different vein, I dropped into Betsy's Hotel in the centre of Tbilisi, a favourite haunt of the British. An Englishman stood at one end of the bar, with beer in one hand and cigarette in the other. He held forth on how best to prepare camel for the table. I caught snippets.

"Has to be a young camel…bury for seven hours." He delivered his culinary tips with such poise and assurance that it was easy to believe the English were forever dining off camel, before moving on to the apple and blackberry crumble and the port.

One frequent haunt has been Kala in Old Tbilisi. There I listen to an old-timer with twinkling eyes play the drums with all the mellow tunefulness of advancing years, while two younger musicians accompany him on cello and piano.

Occasionally female vocalists put in an appearance, seated precariously on a high stool (one at a time, of course). Kala also does a great mint-favoured lemonade, which hits the spot nicely in this heat.

CHAPTER 8

By Horse to Khevsureti

One gap in my knowledge of Georgia was the whole northeast corner, bordering the Russian republics of Dagestan and Chechnya.

To explore this part of the Greater Caucasus meant travelling on one of the worst roads anywhere, venturing beyond the modern world of tarmac, ATMs and wi-fi, but that was part of its charm. Eventually, the exploration also entailed a horse ride, one of the highlights of all my wanderings.

My daughter Rachel, newly graduated in history and Russian, flew out to Tbilisi to join me and on 5 August we set off to the northeast. First we stayed in the lowlands, dillying and dallying a while on the sun-soaked plains of Kakheti, an old kingdom and now Georgia's prime region for wine-growing. The wine, the quiet country charm and some sublime medieval architecture ensure that both the dallying and the dillying in Kakheti are of the highest quality.

We used as our base the historic town of Telavi, one of Georgia's most important medieval trade centres, and checked into a comfortable guesthouse with a garden and a spreading apricot tree.

Naturally we took in a winery but also saw the eleventh-century cathedral of Alaverdi, a tribute to the skills of Georgia's medieval craftsmen. Fifty metres high, for nearly 1,000 years Alaverdi was the highest church in the country. A beautiful building barely known in Western Europe, it has a beguiling simplicity and is bathed in light from sixteen windows in the cupola.

The monastery at Alaverdi has become one of the places leading the renaissance of natural Georgian winemaking. Its website, since1011.com, highlights the fact that the oldest earthenware jars for winemaking found in the monastery date back to the early eleventh century. "Wine heals soul and flesh…" says the monastery's website.

The adventure proper began after Telavi. The idea was to travel in a four-wheel-drive vehicle up to the village of Omalo in the high remote region of Tusheti. The road to Omalo featured in the BBC's television series *World's Most Dangerous Roads.*

Our guesthouse landlady arranged a vehicle for Rachel and myself to travel with two Swiss sisters from Klosters, in their early twenties. In these situations you do weigh up the driver and Levan, a middle-aged veteran of the road to Omalo, looked the business to me.

We headed north across the plain, straight for the hazy wall of mountain ahead of us that was the Caucasus. The landscape held both the greenery of orchards and vineyards and the parched quality of a particularly dry summer – the rivers had very little water flowing. By the roadside were bucketfuls of peaches for sale and a donkey pulled a cart laden with watermelons.

When the road started to climb the tarmac soon disappeared. Up close, the landscape still looked in places rather like a wall of mountain. There were moments when Levan had to switch on his windscreen wipers because water from roadside streams was falling onto the roof of the vehicle. That is a hint that the climb is steep.

We made it to the Abano Pass, at 2,850 metres the highest drivable pass in the Caucasus. Clouds swirled and patches of snow lay on the ground. Most of the year this road is closed.

Four hours after leaving Telavi we pulled into Omalo, a scattered village with lower and upper parts on a broad rising grassland topped by a medieval fortress. Built originally to keep out Mongol invaders, this fortress has benefited in recent years from the generosity of a Dutch couple who have taken the lead in restoring the towers that form the citadel.

This is Big Country, with wide mountain panoramas, pine forests and a powerful feeling of space and isolation. Most Tushetians – the people of Tusheti – head for other homes on the plains when the snow starts to fall in October and leave only a token population to stay in the mountain villages through the winter.

We settled into one of Omalo's guesthouses and entered a little world of holidaymakers who by chance had arrived from several countries to dine at the one table. We sat down for our evening meal with the Swiss sisters Laura and Lisia and a Georgian family living in Kazakhstan's largest city, Almaty.

The evening meal turned into a *supra*, with a toastmaster or *tamada*. And the *supra* turned into a political discussion which laid bare how concerned some Georgians are about their country's future.

The father, a banker called Mamuka Kirvalidze, took it upon himself to be *tamada*. I had been told at my first *supra* in Georgia that the first toast was always to God. "Not so," said Mamuka, adding that in Georgia's southwestern region of Adjara and in the Guria region immediately to the north of Adjara, the first toast was to peace.

"To peace," he said and we all toasted. This might seem a very anodyne and innocent toast, but in today's Georgia it can easily be construed as having geopolitical overtones. Georgia fought and lost a war against Russia in 2008 and since then Georgia's two breakaway regions of Abkhazia and South Ossetia have become increasingly aligned with Moscow.

The big political story out of Georgia in the summer of 2015 has been accusations by the government in Tbilisi that Russia has shifted border markers in South Ossetia to expand the territory. Local Georgian residents say the border has been moved more than one kilometre. Russia has denied moving the markers but the whole issue of Russia's future intentions in Georgia hangs uncomfortably over the country.

At our *supra,* the banker Mamuka was present with his wife, two daughters and teenage son, Zurab. The toast to peace set a very clear tone and Zurab took on the role of ardent patriot, chafing at the bit to become a professional politician and protect his country from the Russians.

"No politics," said father to son at one point. But the elephant in the room – Georgia's future as a nation – was clearly out of its box and could not be put back in again so quickly.

One of the other toasts proposed by Mamuka was to freedom. "To freedom," we all said lustily and everyone knew exactly what the sub-text was here. It was a moving evening, focused on the deep concerns of a nation, which has been invaded and brutalised so many times in its history.

The next day I set out with Rachel and the Swiss sisters to walk north, deeper into Tusheti, to the village of Dartlo. We hiked on a jeep track over slopes forested with pine – Tusheti is a reminder of how beautiful a natural pine forest can be. It is a different thing entirely from a conifer plantation, with trees interspersed with rocks looking like the very essence of a Romantic painting.

Along the way we grazed on wild raspberries growing by the roadside. For the last stretch we walked along a deep valley where the two sides were utterly different – on our southern side of the river the slope was covered with trees while the other vast mountainside opposite us was bare, with shifting herds of sheep.

We walked into Dartlo after more than five hours on the road and the place came as a shock. I had been expecting a sleepy sort of place, but it had a buzz. It seemed to be saying "OK, we're pretty small now, but give us ten years and we'll be a South Caucasus resort of choice."

What a mix of folk! There were Russian bikers, courting couples, French-speaking tourists and down by the river a summer camp of Georgian university students. In the evening they played Frisbee and split logs for the fire. There was a holiday mood, just a few kilometres from the Chechnya border.

To add to the general feeling of activity it was shearing day and four Georgian men were busy with their electric shears, creating a great pile of wool.

You can have absolutely no idea what places are like until you hit the road and visit them. Different places have such different energies. On top of that our own personalities come into play, awarding high or low marks to the places we visit. Dartlo has the buzz of a successful frontier settlement and won an enthusiastic thumbs-up from me.

What I badly wanted to do next was to savour the remote peaks and empty country to the northwest of us. In guidebooks I had read about a five-day walk from Omalo, over to the town of Shatili in the region called Khevsureti. Perhaps I could do it on horseback.

First, after a night in Dartlo, we all walked back to Omalo. My initial attempt to organise this trip to Shatili drew a blank. My guidebook said the Tusheti visitor centre just outside Omalo could help set up guides and horses. Well, on the day I dropped by it couldn't provide even a scrap of information.

As usual, a more serendipitous approach was needed. The day after we came back to Omalo, Rachel and I walked to Shenaqo, a sleepy village a few kilometres east on the other side of a forested canyon. We hiked along a track heavy with the mingled scent of heat, dust and pine.

On our return to Omalo we repaired to a shop cum café. The owner, Eteri Markhvaidze, spoke Russian. Rachel also has good Russian and thanks to her we quickly had a conversation going on how I could do the trek. Eteri knew a man who could be my guide.

She took out a calculator and did the sums. I agreed to pay 50 lari (nearly $22) a day to the guide for six days of hire – a four-day ride to the destination, the village of Shatili, and the guide's two-day ride back. On the same basis I hired two horses at 35 lari (about $15.20) per horse per day. I also hired a tent. The guide, a lean eighteen-year-old named Lasha Arshaulidze, joined us and said he could start the next day.

I bought food for the journey from Eteri – bread, lots of *khachapuri* (Georgia's cheesy bread), tinned fish, gherkins, cheese, Snickers bars and bottled water. The owner of our guesthouse, a kindly woman, insisted on wrapping the food in newspaper to protect it and she turned up pink pages of the *Financial Times* to do the job. Hardly anywhere on this planet is remote any more.

The next morning Rachel climbed on board a four-wheel-drive for the first stage of her journey home and I met up with Lasha. He vaulted onto his mount with all the agility of an Olympic gymnast. I had struggled onto mine with the nimbleness of a Chelsea pensioner and I felt a pang of jealousy.

I was on a nine-year-old chestnut mare of Caucasus stock named Luna. For the next four days she would be the most important being in my life. A foal accompanied Lasha's nameless mare, so we were quite an expedition.

For the second time I covered the ground to Dartlo and on arrival had mild intimations of Groundhog Day – it was shearing day again. We passed Dartlo without stopping.

Lasha and I had agreed to communicate in Russian since he had next to no English. But mid-afternoon he revealed his knowledge of one of the most important words in the English language. "Lunch," he said. And so we lunched. This was our deepest exchange in English.

We rode past the villages of Chesho and Parsma before we reached Girevi, the literal end of the road and our halt for the night. Just beyond the village a Tushetian stone tower stood tall, giving gravitas to the place.

We slept in our tents and the Caucasus night in August was mild, warmer than Wales when I had camped there a few weeks earlier.

Before we set out on day two I presented my passport at Girevi's border police post, an establishment with its own hens. I received a permit to travel to Shatili and off we went, heading northwest into mountains empty of human settlement.

The path soon became challenging. It rose quickly and before I knew it we were hundreds of metres up on a mountainside. To our left was a precipitous drop to the river below. The path was in poor condition, narrow and strewn with loose slivers of stone. Luna was proving herself to be a sure-footed steed, but I still had moments of terror just contemplating where I was and how dependent I was on my horse. One misstep by Luna and neither of us was likely to survive.

By way of welcome diversion we rode through the abandoned village of Chontio, with stone houses on either side now falling down. Deserted villages prompt questions. Why on earth did people build on this remote spot? What did they do in the evenings? Was the death of the village swift or lingering?

We were not always on horseback. On the most difficult sections we dismounted. Sometimes the path ran all the way down to the river, but the predominant story of the day was threading our way high above tumbling waters on the slenderest of paths.

On the first day we had travelled with bottled water, but the rest of the ride we travelled with no water at all. We simply stopped at streams and springs where typically a glass or a cup would stand on stone shelving by the side of the flowing water.

We camped the second night at the Kwachidi bivouac site on the valley floor. Here I could gauge how popular this route has become. There were seven tents with walkers by early evening and then twelve saddled horses rode in from the east with just four riders, Georgians apparently on a mission to pick up tourists or their gear.

Next morning I talked to one of the hikers, a young Englishman with a stout stick setting out to walk the path we had taken the previous day. He introduced himself as David Hirtenstein from Oxford and said that he was walking to India. He had begun his journey in Italy in October 2013 and expected to reach India in a few years.

He was trying to travel without money. "So how does that work?" I asked. "I just don't worry," replied David, who has a blog at atasteofancientroutes.wordpress.com. David's father, Stephen, is a world-leading scholar on the medieval Sufi mystic Ibn 'Arabi.

The encounter with David was frustratingly brief. We spoke for only fifteen minutes or so, but I got a very clear sense that I was meeting a remarkable man. It enriches our world to have people like David who want to spend years hiking the trails of the world. This kind of experience gives breadth and depth to a human life. When David writes the book of his travels I feel sure it will be every bit as exceptional as the man.

On day three we climbed to the Atsunta Pass, 3,431 metres high. It was a hot, sticky ascent, sometimes on horseback, sometimes on foot, and the latter stages were through a lunar landscape of rocks and scree.

After the pass we had a steep scramble down by foot and soon we were back in a greener world. We rode on a very steep mountainside covered with stumpy rhododendron bushes and I tried out David's mantra – I just don't worry.

We emerged onto a grassy plateau with 360-degree views of the Caucasus, with the snow-capped Mount Tebulos, part of the Chechnya border range, off to our right. Two hawks hovered just ahead of us and one after another dived for prey. I felt part of the landscape, completely at one with the world around me. At the same time it was the closest to heaven I have ever been on this earth. Perhaps it was an experience of what Sufis call 'oneness'.

We camped the night close by the Khidotani police border post.

On the final morning I received my marching orders from Lasha. "One hour on foot," he said. This sounded ominous and I braced for the worst. But in the event there were no yawning chasms this time, just a rather steep descent. We led our horses down through a lovely deciduous woodland with a variety of flowers, some overhanging the path.

At moments like this I longed for the company of a Caucasus version of Edward Thomas to tell me about all the different flowers.

We reached the valley bottom and were back in the land of jeep tracks and human settlement. We rode on a track following a stream and came to Khonischala, with neat vegetable patches and solar energy. It was the first village we had seen since leaving Girevi two days earlier.

As we rode through, three young women each with a tin bucket crossed the road in front of us. This type of image is so sharp when you have been away from humankind even for just two days.

A few kilometres further on we came to Mutso, a deserted old town on a pinnacle of rock. I climbed up and gazed into a stone crypt where during outbreaks of plague the dying came to live out their last days or hours. You can still see human bones inside. Georgians know that Mutso is no ordinary place and renovation work began here in 2014.

We rode on to more stone crypts with human remains set above a gorge at a place called Anatori. From here a Russian flag is visible a few hundred metres away. During these latest Caucasus travels I met the military attaché of an EU member state and he asserted that the flag is on Georgian soil.

In late afternoon, after riding about ninety kilometres in all, we rounded a bend and there was Shatili, a magnificent collection of interlinked stone towers built between the seventh and thirteenth centuries on a rocky hill. People moved out of them in the second half of the twentieth century and most are now empty. A small new village has been built next door, powered by electricity from a little hydro plant on the Argun river.

Over a beer in the evening, Lasha told me that neither Luna nor his horse had ever travelled on the path to Shatili before. He was probably right not to have troubled me with that detail earlier.

Shatili is in the sparsely populated region of Khevsureti. According to Georgia's official tourist literature, the men in Khevsureti wore chainmail armour and carried swords right up to the 1930s. Georgia has certainly marched to its own drum!

A little book called *Caucasian Paths: Khevsureti* has provided me with more insights into the ways of old Khevsureti. It says that up to the middle of the twentieth century the region had a sexual custom called *stsorproba*. A young unmarried couple were allowed to lie together during the night, but caresses below the waist were forbidden and a sword was placed between them. What is this Khevsur thing about swords?

During my visit to Shatili my one encounter with local culture was an outdoor concert of Khevsuretian music. On a stage in front of the old town, a four-woman group in traditional attire sang and played on string instruments and drums. The music had a strong emotional charge and often a tinge of sadness, but it was vibrant and good entertainment.

I have now made three trips to the Greater Caucasus range in northern Georgia. The learning at a personal level is that this travelling has done me the world of good. I have breathed the pure air of the mountains, seen extraordinary places and had a sense of living – sometimes quite literally – on the edge. I feel alive to the tips of my fingers.

When I sit in a Tbilisi café, I feel blessed that I have seen what French friends would probably call *la Géorgie profonde*.

I have seen the great mountain ranges that separate Georgia from Russia and watched a Georgian border guard train his binoculars on the giant neighbour to the north. But paradoxically I have a stronger sense now of Georgia's vulnerability. This watchfulness by the guard is little more than theatre. If the northern neighbours really want to play rough they already have forces in South Ossetia, close to the very heartland of Georgia. They also have troops in Armenia to the south.

My crystal ball is dim. Right now things are calm and I have no hesitation in claiming that Omalo to Shatili is one of the great trails of the world.

CHAPTER 9

One Georgian's Perspective on Georgia

Russia looms large in Georgia. Back in Tbilisi, it features prominently in a conversation I have with a friend, Moscow-born Alexander Janiashvili.

Alexander is a young Georgian patriot and entrepreneur who wants to see his country take a tougher line with the powerful neighbour to the north. Thirty-two-year-old Alexander is a man of unusual energy who often starts his working day flipping pancakes for guests at the Pushkin 10 hostel he co-owns in the heart of Tbilisi. Between twenty and thirty percent of his guests are from Russia.

After breakfast he puts on business attire and heads off to his other job, working as a petroleum geologist at a small Georgian company in the oil sector. A tall, dark-haired man with presence, Alexander says he puts in about eight hours a day at each of his two workplaces. What it is to be young.

Born in Moscow where his father stayed on after studying, he spent the first twenty-six years of his life there but is now settled in Tbilisi. Given his knowledge of both Georgia and Russia, I wanted to get his perspective on the state of his country, whose affairs seem still to be enmeshed with its big neighbour. I made the questions very open, to see where the conversation flowed.

"How is Georgia doing?" I asked. The answer came slowly, after what seemed like painful reflection. "I wish it was doing better," said Alexander, adding, "I am a big patriot of Georgia, a big supporter of Georgia. I love Georgia, that is why I am here, that is why I moved to Georgia because I wanted to make something good, maybe, for my country."

One general difficulty, he said, was the small scale of the country's market. "I moved from Moscow and it's nothing. The whole of Georgia's population is like only a quarter of Moscow's population."

We soon moved on to thornier matters of Georgian politics and international relations. In my experience, many a conversation about Georgia's path leads to a focus on one name – Mikheil Saakashvili. The conversation with Alexander was no exception. Saakashvili led the Rose Revolution of 2003 that brought Soviet-era leadership in Georgia to an end. He was president from 2004 until 2013 and won plaudits for his campaigns against crime and corruption. He is an arch-foe of Vladimir Putin, who once said he wanted to hang Saakashvili "by the balls".

I asked Alexander how he saw relations with Russia evolving. Russia beat Georgia in a war in 2008 and Georgia's breakaway regions of Abkhazia and South Ossetia are now aligned with Moscow. Many Georgians would say they are effectively occupied by Russia.

Alexander replied, "One of the best things that Saakashvili did during his presidency, that you could not imagine before, was that Georgia became really independent of Russia, absolutely independent. Before we were very dependent on the trading with Russia, our wine, agriculture. We were getting gas from there and many Georgians worked there sending money to here and gradually they (the Saakashvili government) closed visas – we can't go there, we can't trade with there. We started getting gas from Azerbaijan, zero from Russia. So we could survive without this.

"And now after this year, after this occupation we don't need to compromise anything, we don't need it. This new government promised they would improve relations with Russia – which never works with Russia. If you stop annoying it they only start moving their occupation borders inside the country."

Alexander said he believed the Georgian government was following Russian instructions.

"They are just sitting and doing what their chief wants," said Alexander. And who is their chief? "Ultimately Ivanishvili, Bidzina Ivanishvili."

Ivanishvili is a Georgian billionaire who made his fortune in Russia in the era of privatisation, mainly during the rule of Boris Yeltsin in the 1990s when Russian state assets were sold off cheap and a few individuals hit the jackpot. Ivanishvili founded and led the Georgian Dream coalition which took on Saakashvili's party in the polls and defeated it. In one early round of political sparring between the two men, Saakashvili's government deprived Ivanishvili of his Georgian citizenship.

Ivanishvili has for years faced accusations that he is a stooge of Russia. He denies this and says that he himself is critical of Putin. He depicted his campaigning against Saakashvili as an attempt to rescue Georgia from a government that was increasingly authoritarian.

Saakashvili is now banished from Georgian politics. He is wanted in his own country on charges of abuse of power, but he says these charges are politically motivated. In 2015 the Ukrainian government appointed Saakashvili governor of Odessa (he held this post until 2016 when he resigned and accused Ukrainian President Petro Poroshenko of corruption).

Alexander accused the Georgian Dream government of wholesale inactivity. "They didn't do for three years anything," he said. "They keep criticising the previous government which did a lot for the country. The country changed completely."

"People forget what was Georgia before Saakashvili, and what it became, because they start forgetting, taking it for granted," said Alexander. "They don't remember that we didn't have electricity... the next day when he came the electricity was twenty-four hours. He killed corruption, he changed police. Before people were afraid of police, they hated them. Now the police started having a very good reputation. He killed crime, because when you don't have corruption you don't have crime. Tbilisi became, according to researchers, the number one city in Europe where women feel safe."

Alexander added, "Also he was pushing on education... he brought 10,000 English speakers to the country [to teach the language]."

Alexander said he had heard from an American involved in the programme that only sixty-five of these native English speakers were still working in the country.

My conversation with Alexander highlighted a singular truth about Georgian politics. The country has a president and a prime minister but Georgians barely mention them. Somehow they are not rated as very important. Georgians talk about Saakashvili, who is banished from the country, and Ivanishvili, who is the richest man in the land but has no position in the government. These two men and the feud between them do much to shape the whole emotional field of national politics.

Finally I asked Alexander about his 'high dream' for his country, what would be the best scenario?

He talked about the need, as he saw it, for Georgians to take more responsibility for their own lives. He said many of his compatriots wanted the occupied territories of Abkhazia and South Ossetia to be reunited with Georgia. For this to happen, he believed Georgia had to work on becoming a more attractive place.

"I think we should deserve it. We should become more attractive for them," he said.

Alexander is not alone in feeling that Georgia could be doing better, but his hostel and the wider tourism industry are doing well.

At his Pushkin 10 hostel, tourists from the former Soviet Union rub shoulders with Westerners and both Russian and English are heard over breakfast as those pancakes arrive at the table. It is a stimulating place to be.

If you come by the hostel in early June, you'll even get the chance of a party with a high cultural tone. Pushkin 10 celebrates the birthday of the great Russian poet, author of *Eugene Onegin*, born on 6 June, 1799.

CHAPTER 10

To the Land of Fire

I feel very comfortable in Tbilisi; in some moods I could stay here forever. But my aim is to see the three countries of the South Caucasus, not just Georgia, so I must move on.

I gird my loins and repair to the Azerbaijan consulate to apply for a visa. In the Caucasus, Azerbaijan is a byword for corruption and I can see why even before I set foot in the country. Azerbaijan is the only one of the South Caucasus states, which requires British citizens to have a visa, and the consulate informs me that mine will cost $118. Ouch!

To rub salt in the wound, the consulate guides travellers to a Mr Fixit who has an office right by the consulate and charges a small fee for a few little formalities. The authorities demand to see a hotel reservation. So Mr Fixit produces a piece of paper saying that I am booked into one double room at Baku's most expensive hotel, along with an Italian gentleman sitting opposite me in his office.

I have never seen the Italian before. The hotel booking palaver is a moneymaking nonsense – we are not required in real life to go anywhere near the hotel or pay it a cent. These little games leave a bad taste in my mouth and serve to shape my attitude towards the government in Baku.

(In the 2015 Corruption Perceptions Index of Transparency International, a non-government body that campaigns for a world free of corruption, I saw that Azerbaijan stood in 119th position, against Georgia's ranking of forty-eighth and Armenia's ninety-fifth. The least corrupt countries are at the top of the list. Transparency International listed Azerbaijan as one of the countries "restricting, if not totally stifling, civil society and free media – both proven to prevent corruption".)

Anyway, with visa in hand I made my travel arrangements. I bought a train ticket at Tbilisi Central a day ahead and chose second class for 60 lari ($26). Three classes of travel were on offer and with my ticket I would get a place in a four-berth sleeper.

If your idea of a train journey is to travel in style, with a dining car and no border formalities, never take the night train from Tbilisi to Baku.

Who knows whether the European Union's Schengen borderless zone will survive, but right now travellers in Europe are spoilt. Going by train in April from Poland to Slovakia I didn't know when I had left one and entered the other. Travelling from Tbilisi to Baku, the capital of Azerbaijan, is a different story.

Train journeys always say something about a country's priorities. Tbilisi Central is not in great shape. The platforms look as if they were hit years ago by slight earth tremors and never repaired.

The train, with carriages painted cream and green, left smack on time at 4:30pm. The timetable listed fifty stops (yes, *fifty*) between Tbilisi and Baku. Not an express train then. Travelling time was scheduled to be fourteen hours and forty minutes to cover 551 kilometres. My companions were three affable Azeri young men who told me that Baku was much nicer than Tbilisi.

There was no dining or buffet car, but when we arrived at the Georgian border we were able to buy drinks and snacks at little

Out and about in nighttime Baku

shops in the station, where we had a one-hour scheduled stop. Then we moved slowly to the Azerbaijan border where we had another scheduled sixty-minute stop. One border guard took my photo and another rummaged through my luggage, paying particular attention to reading matter in the best traditions of a police state.

At the Azerbaijan border it was pretty warm on the train, being August, and I went into the corridor at one point to get some air. A train stewardess whom I nicknamed the Gulag Guard brusquely ordered me to sit down in my compartment. Not wishing to create an international incident I complied, but soon the corridor filled with sweat-soaked passengers yearning to be cool.

Eventually we got through the border and had some sleep under spotless bedclothes, but hours before arriving in Baku the Gulag Guard knocked on our doors and insisted that we rise so that she could gather the bedclothes.

The view outside was of scrub and low brown hills. The final approach to Baku was the best bit of the journey. The Caspian Sea came into view on the right of the train and on the left for a while was a lake with petrels, I think, swooping low over the water. Scattered over the landscape on both sides of us were dozens of 'nodding donkeys' pumping oil. Very atmospheric!

We arrived in Baku one hour and five minutes late. I am glad I did the train ride, but once was enough. Taxis take half the time and if costs are shared are not very much more expensive.

Baku, on the shores of the Caspian Sea, is an elegant modern capital with glittering buildings that pierce the sky. Looking at the futuristic Flame Towers, all sinuous curves and bright lights, you expect a city with buzz.

But somehow the buzz just isn't there. Where are the buskers, the beggars, the clamorous moments of big-city life? Baku, or Baki as the locals call it, is agreeable and modern, fresh from its successful hosting of the European Games in June. But something isn't quite right, something is missing.

I think it is a little concept called freedom of speech. I picked up quickly that self-censorship was in the air. You just breathed it in, along with the aroma of your morning coffee.

Baku is a most friendly and courteous city, with a splendid tree-lined promenade by the Caspian Sea to enchant the visitor. It is a physically handsome city and you can eat and drink well. But it's not a place where you stand on a soapbox and denounce the government. Or if you do, you bear in mind that such behaviour could land you behind bars.

Sorting out my reactions to Baku, which felt to me as if it were under sedation, I started to read news stories about Azerbaijan. They were both illuminating and depressing.

The New York-based Committee to Protect Journalists rated Azerbaijan as the fifth most censored country in the world, after

Eritrea, North Korea, Saudi Arabia and Ethiopia. In other words, the committee sees Azerbaijan's media as the most repressed anywhere in the former Soviet Union. That is quite an achievement; it beats some stiff competition.

Here is a chronology of some events concerning Azeri journalists and human rights activists in 2015.

June – Opposition journalist Emin Huseynov, director of the Institute for Reporters' Freedom and Safety, flees the country after taking refuge for months in the Swiss embassy. He flies out on the plane of the Swiss foreign minister.

9 August – Huseynov's successor as head of the institute, journalist Rasim Aliyev, dies of injuries in a Baku hospital after being severely beaten by a group of people the previous day. Officials link the death to criticism of a football player, but human rights watchdogs say it could have been prompted by photos he posted online of police brutality and social deprivation.

13 August – Leading human rights activists Leyla and Arif Yunus are jailed on charges which include fraud and tax evasion. Leyla, director of the Institute of Peace and Democracy, is jailed for eight-and-a-half years, her husband Arif, a well-known historian, for seven years. Both have severe health problems.

1 September – Prominent journalist Khadija Ismayilova is jailed for seven-and-a-half years on charges that include tax evasion and illegal business activities. Ismayilova, who worked for the US government-financed Radio Free Europe/Radio Liberty, is known for her work exposing corruption in the Azeri elite and reporting on the business dealings of President Ilham Aliev. During her trial, Ismayilova describes the government of President Aliev as a "repression machine".

President Aliev inherited his post from his father, Heidar Aliev, who dominated the politics of his country for decades and once headed the KGB in Azerbaijan. The president has set out his views on the core values of good journalism in a book entitled *I Challenge the Journalists to Patriotism.*

The president himself is very patriotic. You can tell because up and down the land are big portraits of him posing next to the national flag. Sometimes these portraits have a fetching stone surround. This makes them look rather like shrines, which I suppose is exactly what they are meant to be.

It is the good fortune of the president and the misfortune of Azerbaijan's bloodied human rights movement that the country is rich in oil and gas. This was one of the places where the modern oil industry was born, in the nineteenth century, and it still has large reserves. Azerbaijan does business with Western oil companies and has been polishing a Western image, but it has jailed so many of its pro-Western intellectuals that this posturing looks hollow.

Writing in *Foreign Affairs* magazine in 2014, Caucasus expert Thomas de Waal said that Azerbaijan had embarked on the biggest human rights crackdown in wider Europe. He said an estimated ninety-eight political prisoners were in jail.

Fuelled by its oil wealth, Azerbaijan has also gone on an arms-buying spree. In a war with Armenia in the early 1990s, Azerbaijan lost about 20,000 dead and nearly fourteen percent of its internationally recognised territory. This was the region of Nagorno-Karabakh and some other adjacent areas. Baku's proclaimed aim is to win this territory back and it has been buying attack aircraft, artillery systems, surface-to-air missiles and drones from Israel, Pakistan and Russia.

I did not bring up the subject of politics with Azeris I met in Baku and I let them inquire about matters that interested them. What did I think of Azeri women? What are British women like? What do they drink? How big is my pension?

All the Azeris I met unfailingly showed me kindness. But the buttoned-up quality of the place would have tested me had I stayed for long. It is striking how quickly the outsider conforms to the habit of self-censorship. When foreign travellers in Baku discuss Armenia their voices drop to a whisper. It's that kind of subject; it's that kind of place.

Azerbaijan, in both its past and its present, packs surprises. Perhaps the biggest surprise to me was that once upon a time it contained a Christian kingdom, known to historians as Caucasian Albania (no relation to the Balkan state). When the Romans first pushed into the Caucasus in the first century BC, they called people they found in what is now Azerbaijan Albanians. These people converted to Christianity from the fourth century and by the time of the Arab invasions of the tenth century were blending in with other ethnic groups around them.

Some of their decayed churches still survive and when British author Brigid Keenan travelled in northern Azerbaijan just a few years ago she was told that their ruined monasteries are still there in the forests.

In modern times, after the Russian Revolution of 1917, the tsarist empire fell apart and the South Caucasus region was briefly home to three independent states. The Democratic Republic of Azerbaijan became the first parliamentary democracy in the Muslim world and Azeri women won the vote earlier than their British sisters.

Azerbaijan today is a Shi'ite-majority state but you really wouldn't guess that when walking the streets of Baku. Muslim attire for women is the exception and in a city-centre square there is a statue of a young woman sporting tightly fitting jeans, a bare midriff and a fairly minimalist top. She is talking on her mobile phone, has a handbag slung over a shoulder and generally looks the epitome of the modern material girl. Baku is a modern material city and in that sense the statue fits right in. But it still struck me as odd.

One delightful surprise for me, after I had started to focus on the South Caucasus, was to discover the great Azerbaijan novel *Ali and Nino*. This book, published first in Vienna in German in 1937, is a beautifully written tale of love, war and cultural tensions, sometimes funny, sometimes sad, but always totally engaging.

It moves to a number of locations from Baku's Old City to a simple village in the Caucasus uplands, from Nagorno-Karabakh to Tbilisi and Tehran, and there is always a deep sense of place. At the heart of the story is the love between Ali, a proud Shi'ite Muslim from Baku, and his spirited bride, a Georgian princess called Nino. Ali loves the desert and his soul belongs to the east. Nino has the same name as the saint who converted Georgia to Christianity and she is an emancipated woman of the West.

The novel was written under the pseudonym Kurban Said and there has been much debate about the identity of the author, but the majority view seems to favour Lev Nussimbaum, an ethnic Jew who said that he had converted to Islam.

Just a few weeks after my visit to Baku, my old friend Laurence Purcell went to the Azeri capital on a short holiday. (He it was who inspired me to embark on my Caucasus travels when he took a brief visit to Georgia in 2014.) Laurence reported that he and his travelling companion hired a guide to show them the Abşeron Peninsula near Baku.

The guide, a well-educated woman of about thirty, sat with Laurence in a sculpture park and regaled him with an account of how she was writing a novel as a kind of counter-blast to *Ali and Nino*. She was greatly affronted, he said, by the idea of a Georgian girl being more beautiful than an Azeri one. So both hero and heroine, in her book, would be Azeri Muslims. It is a bit like rewriting *Romeo and Juliet* so that both of the lovers are Capulets. But Laurence's conversation in the sculpture park did seem to shed light on changing moods in Azerbaijan.

Having spent $118 for my Azerbaijan visa I must get my money's worth and see the country. Keeping the Caucasus theme forefront, I decide to head north to the mountains and the border with Dagestan.

In Baku I meet Mark Elliott, author of a well-regarded guidebook to Azerbaijan. Mark knows his stuff and he tells me that the government has effectively closed some of the country's loveliest walking trails to foreigners. You have to get one permission from here and another from there and in real life hardly anyone bothers to try.

Azerbaijan does market itself as a tourist destination, describing itself as the Land of Fire, but I never sensed any fire in the belly of Baku's tourist offices. The Land of Fire tag has a historical pedigree. Certainly Azerbaijan has mud volcanoes, naturally occurring vents of gas with flames leaping in the air and a history of fire-worshipping Zoroastrians.

Mark suggests I travel to the remote border town of Sudur, which *is* a permissible journey, so I make that my destination. I take a shared taxi through arid scrubland to the town of Quba. This is a bustling place with a market noteworthy for mountains of watermelons and fish swimming in bathtubs. Just across the river is a celebrated town that I am curious to see. In Soviet times it was called Krasnaya Sloboda, but today it goes by the name of Qirmizi Qesebe.

This is the last outpost of Mountain Jews, in the middle of a country where the majority religion is Shi'ite Islam. The Mountain Jews have an oral tradition that claims they are descended from the Ten Lost Tribes of Ancient Israel. They are thought to have travelled to Persia as early as the eighth century BC and to have settled in the Caucasus by the fifth century AD.

I visit on a cloudy day with sporadic drizzle and wander through nearly empty streets to the melancholy sound of water dripping onto guttering. An old man with a walking stick crosses my path. I turn left and a little way down the street two elderly women with headscarves sit in front of their homes chatting. In the centre of town, this is as lively as it gets.

I feel linguistically challenged in Qirmizi Qesebe where the main language is Juhuri, a form of Persian. There is no traffic and barely any commerce, but I finally see one shop open and go in. The shopkeeper has no Russian so I just open my arms wide and say plaintively "Where is everyone? Israel?"

"Moscow, Israel," comes the reply. It is clear that considerable sums of money have been invested in this town. There are many ostentatious mansions, but unlike its neighbour on the other side of the river this place is very, very quiet. Eventually I meet two young boys from Moscow who are here on holiday. In winter, they tell me, Qirmizi Qesebe is even quieter.

The gravitational pull of Israel and the withering of Jewish communities in the Muslim world is by now a stale story. Still, it is an emotional experience to walk the streets of a town where life is draining away. The population today has dropped to fewer than 4,000, compared with 18,000 in Soviet times.

After a night in Quba I press on northward by bus to a town called Qusare. I am now deep into a region where the main language is Lezgin or Lezgian. In the Caucasus, there is such a mosaic of languages that it is hard to keep up. Lezgin is an important Caucasus language, with about 800,000 speakers, mainly in the Russian republic of Dagestan and northeast Azerbaijan.

Author Clive James has proposed that poisonous Australian snakes be divided into three categories, starting with lethal and going up to absolutely ridiculous. If a similar system were used for the difficulty of languages, then Lezgin would surely be deemed absolutely ridiculous. It has eighteen grammatical cases for its nouns. If it were not for Russian, travellers in the Caucasus would have few options but sign language or silence.

In Qusare I take a taxi for the final leg of my journey, to the border village of Sudur. Very soon Dagestan comes into view, a string of villages on the other side of the Samur river. So near yet so far! I am in effect triply barred from entering Dagestan. I have no Russian visa, there is no border crossing here and my government says Dagestan is dangerous because of a low-level Islamist insurgency.

We leave a metalled road behind and travel along a muddy track through mountainous country. But soon cloud envelops us and rain starts to fall. After about two-and-a-half hours out in the Azeri countryside in the mud, mist and rain, my Russian-speaking driver says he will go no further. His ageing Zhiguli car can take no more.

Soon a knight in shining armour comes out of the mist, riding a beaten-up jeep. The name of my rescuer is Zagid. He takes me the remaining six kilometres to Sudur and invites me to stay with his family.

Zagid Askerov is a kind, thoughtful man in his mid-forties. He speaks three languages, Lezgin, Azeri and Russian, and owns three cows. He and his wife Ilgame are small subsistence farmers and they have a teenage daughter and two sons, one of whom is at university. Their home is simple but cosy, with all the accommodation on an upper floor.

For dinner on my first evening we sit down to fresh plums and

My host on the Azerbaijan/Dagestan border

grapes, followed by a hearty beef and potato stew, washed down with tea. This family feels like my one real connection in Azerbaijan and I talk to Zagid about many things. All three of his brothers, he tells me, live and work in Dagestan and he has no time for the official Western view that travel there is risky.

"There are a few bandits," he says. "But don't you have any bandits in Britain?" He gets his news off Russian television and is informed. At one point we get onto the subject of Scotland's 2014 independence referendum and I say independence was rejected but I can't remember the voting figures.

"It was fifty-five percent to forty-five percent," says Zagid. Checking later I see that this is the correct figure. Zagid has brought me up-to-date on the level of political awareness in the back lands of northern Azerbaijan.

The next morning the mist rises and I discover that Sudur is perched on the northern side of a dramatic canyon which drops down to a river of the same name. It is a glorious spot. For the first time in my life I see a whole group of eagles, perhaps five or six, wheeling in the skies above the canyon. Over to the southwest, the great hunk of mountain that is Shahdagh is now in view, with snow on the 4,243-metre peak.

After we have admired the views Zagid shows me the whitewashed village school, which has about sixty-five pupils. His daughter, fifteen-year-old Amina, is one of them and she wants to be a physics teacher.

In conversations with me Amina has been applying the classic British technique of speaking very slowly and loudly, but in Russian. This approach does make me feel slightly retarded.

What to do now with this man who has arrived out of the blue? Zagid asks if I would like to watch a video of a wedding that took place in Sudur in June. A traveller has to be open to experience so I say, "That would be lovely."

The bride, an eighteen-year-old with long dark hair piled high, first wore blue, then orange and finally white. This is a seriously long wedding video and it focuses mainly on the guests dancing to live music. They throw money for the musicians and little boys scamper and collect it.

There are lots of outstretched arms and much nifty footwork. Men dance with men, women with women and men with women. There are also virtuoso solo acts. The connecting thread is a total lack of self-consciousness. This is what keeps me watching. Young and old, fat and thin, handsome and ugly all dance without any sense of awkwardness. What a beautiful celebration!

CHAPTER 11

Armenia Packs a Punch

After watching that wedding video on the Azerbaijan–Dagestan border, I followed a very winding road. My priority was to go to a real wedding in Wales, where some dear friends, a groom from the Rhondda and a bride from the United States, were tying the knot. I went back to Baku on the Caspian Sea, then taxis to Tbilisi, a flight home for outdoor nuptials in the Welsh sunshine and back to Georgia.

Shortly after my return to Tbilisi I met up with my godson Tom, who had been with me in Riga and now joined me for some Caucasus travel. We took a *marshrutka* to Yerevan, the Armenian capital.

Armenia is an ancient nation with much to offer the world, but I immediately sensed that it is grappling with some mighty demons. I find that visiting Armenia requires of me a certain amount of emotional heavy lifting. I remind myself occasionally that I am not here to solve the country's problems.

One significant demon is the whole phenomenon of emigration. While Europe faces the conundrum of how to absorb great waves of migrants, Armenia has the opposite challenge – how to persuade people to stay. The population has shrunk from 3.6 million in 1991 to three million today. Less than a third of the world's Armenians live in Armenia.

If you are in a tough neighbourhood, as Armenia is, a falling population is not what you want. Enemies, and the country does have enemies, can seize upon it as a sign of weakness.

Going from Georgia to Armenia, the traveller swaps one indecipherable alphabet for another indecipherable alphabet. (Only Azerbaijan in the South Caucasus uses the Roman script and they got there by a roundabout route. The script changed from Arabic to Roman in the 1920s, to Cyrillic in the 1930s and then back to Roman in the 1990s. Pity the twentieth-century scribes of Azerbaijan!)

The Armenian alphabet was introduced in AD 405 by the linguist and church leader Saint Mesrop Mashtots in order to translate the Bible into Armenian. Yerevan's main avenue is named after him and the general view is that Mashtots was one of the pivotal figures in Armenian history.

His alphabet provided Armenia with a cultural anchor of the highest importance. Armenians have been through trials which make the hair stand on end just to read about them and the patch of earth which they call their own has shifted and shrunk.

But the nation has endured, thanks in large part to a culture based on the book, something you can take with you to a new land. It has even exported its alphabet, since thousands of books written in the Turkish and Kurdish languages have used the Armenian script.

According to Armenian tradition, the whole of humanity spoke Armenian before the linguistic hydra spawned by the Tower of Babel. Oral tradition taught this version of language history for generation after generation – Armenians still living learned it at their grandmother's knee.

So, a new alphabet and for me a new city. Yerevan. This city is older than Rome, but you would never guess that to look at it. Today it is a bustling modern city with a Western pulse and the most impressive traffic jams of the South Caucasus.

Yerevan's history dates back to 782 BC, when king Argishti I established a fortress at Erebuni. This is one of the oldest continuously inhabited cities on earth. One way to connect with Armenia's deep past is to visit Yerevan's extraordinary Matenadaran, one of the most important depositories of ancient books and illuminated manuscripts anywhere in the world.

In modern times, Yerevan had a Persian character and a mainly Muslim population until the First World War. It became Armenian in flavour after the exodus of Armenians fleeing the mass killings perpetrated in Anatolia by Ottoman Turks. Armenia knows these killings as the Genocide and Yerevan is full of billboards marking the centenary. A later chapter will focus on these horrific events because they loom so large in Armenia's history.

The architectural tone of Yerevan is twentieth century and the building material of choice is pink tufa, rock made from volcanic ash.

After arrival we had a mini-tour of the city centre, kindly conducted by an Armenian. Vahagn Petrosyan, a professional interpreter, took us first to the Cascade, a giant stairway built in the 1970s with several levels of sculptures and fountains. By climbing the stairs, on a clear day you get views of Mount Ararat, 5,137 metres high and a defining symbol of Armenia even though it rises on Turkish soil. (Incidentally the border with Turkey is closed, so quick trips to nearby Ararat are out.)

Next Vahagn took us to the central Republic Square, where dancing fountains and music are the city's signature attractions of an evening. Nothing old was on the itinerary for the simple reason that nearly everything old has been bulldozed.

"The city is nearly 3,000 years old, but few of the buildings go back more than 100 years," said Vahagn.

The architecture is European, much of it early Soviet, but in

Yerevan I suddenly felt that the Middle East was not far away. As the vulture flies, the killing fields of northern Syria are not much closer to Yerevan (about 670 kilometres) than to Tbilisi (about 810 kilometres) but Armenia feels closer, culturally and psychologically, to the Middle East than does Georgia.

Today Armenia is a landlocked country, but once upon a time more than 700 years ago, it had a Mediterranean shore. The music and the food of Armenia are partly Middle Eastern in flavour. The *oud*, a pear-shaped string instrument, is important in Arab and in Armenian music.

War in Arab lands hits home emotionally in Armenia, but does not seem to have been a driver of emigration. Indeed, Arab wars have worked the other way – some Armenians from Syria and Iraq have settled in Armenia in recent years.

Yerevan has a distinctive quality of its own, with lots of street life, classy jazz clubs and good people-watching.

A few months earlier, in a Tbilisi hostel, I had met a young Japanese man who had just been in Yerevan. He explained to a group of us why he had crossed the whole of Asia to visit the city. At school in Japan, he said, his female geography teacher, had impressed upon him that the women of Armenia were beautiful. For eight years he held the dream of going to Armenia to see for himself. Finally he got there and with their permission he photographed a number of Armenian women out and about in the capital.

It was a singular tale, but the Japanese traveller exuded the air of a man who had climbed his personal Everest and known the joy of fulfilment.

Admiring the beauty of the women is surely a part of the Yerevan experience. Some common sense is needed here – no city has only beautiful people. But there are enough women in Yerevan who turn heads that silence on the matter would be eccentric.

Quite often you see the classic Armenian look – patrician nose, flowing black hair, perfect posture.

Armenian women, and their sisters in Georgia and Azerbaijan, have remembered what it is to be feminine. They also operate, at least in theory, on a values system which is different from the one which has evolved in the more freewheeling West. The sexual revolution ran out of steaminess somewhere before the Caucasus and their societies, Christian and Muslim alike, are conservative. An ice-maiden hauteur can, of course, enhance the charms that nature has given.

Anyway, we did move on from Yerevan, in case you were wondering, and we hit the road to Armenia's southernmost point, to the border with Iran. We left the city in a shared taxi and very soon had a snapshot of the difficulties of life out in the countryside.

Our taxi ground to a halt, still in full view of Mount Ararat. All travellers on the road, the main artery to the south, were being obstructed by grape farmers, unhappy about the price they were being offered for their produce after a bumper harvest.

About 100 people, farmers and motorists, milled around on the road. Police were present but refrained from strong-arm tactics. A man in suit and tie appeared and talked to the gum-booted farmers. I don't know what he said, but after about forty minutes at a standstill the traffic flowed again.

Protests by grape farmers in Ararat province are something of an annual ritual in September, when the grapes are harvested. Travelling through the Armenian countryside I did not pick up the whiff of prosperity. Lack of economic opportunity is clearly one driver of emigration.

We drove about 250 kilometres through largely barren, sparsely populated hill country to the southern town of Goris, whose population has been steadily falling in recent years. Here we broke our journey and checked into a B&B buzzing with travellers from the Netherlands, Germany and China.

Most of us dined together. The Dutch tourists were two brothers, young adults, born of an Armenian father and Dutch mother and making their first visit to Armenia. They too were engaged in what I called earlier emotional heavy lifting.

I talked mainly to one brother, Levon Goceryan, born in Delft. He already had some opinions on Armenia.

"Their culture is about suffering. Nine out of ten conversations with Armenians are about the Genocide," said Levon. "What I miss is the future focus." Well, you can't be any clearer than that. Whether you have Armenian blood or not, this country certainly gives food for thought.

One of Levon's themes was that Yerevan, unlike the big cities of Western Europe, lacked a youth sub-culture. He felt that Armenian youth simply copied their parents and this stunted innovation.

The next day Tom and I headed south again through the mountains of the Lesser Caucasus, in two *marshrutky* and a taxi, to the stunning town of Meghri close to the frontier with Iran.

Meghri is a perfect destination for lovers of the desert. It is girt by utterly arid lunar mountains, but the town itself is an oasis with extensive apple orchards. This is a landscape of Western Asia. We found accommodation in a house with lime trees in the garden and figs drying on the balcony.

From Meghri we drove out to the border with Iran. This was an external border of the former Soviet Union and for all the world it still looks like a Cold War frontier, with high watchtowers and a barbed wire fence. Over on the other side of the river is Iran, neighbour also to Afghanistan and Pakistan.

This is the southernmost point of my Caucasus journey.

CHAPTER 12

A Hike through Nagorno-Karabakh

In the eyes of the world, the Republic of Nagorno-Karabakh does not exist. That doesn't prevent about 145,000 people from regarding it as their home, nor does it stop men from dying to protect it.

Karabakh is a self-declared republic, unrecognised internationally. It is inhabited by Armenians who in a bloody feat of arms wrested it from Azerbaijan in the early 1990s. The conflict over this beguilingly beautiful region is unresolved and occasionally claims lives on the ceasefire line where Armenian and Azerbaijani forces still spit hate. The government in Baku has vowed to win this land back.

I put Karabakh on my itinerary because this conflict looms so large in the Caucasus. I wanted to feel the pulse of the place and talk to Karabakhtis.

To give structure to our visit I suggested hiking a ten-day section of the Janapar Trail. Tom signed up for this and we made a good team. Tom was navigator and I was interpreter. In the countryside of Karabakh, English is almost as exotic a language as Welsh. People speak the Karabakh dialect of Armenian and also Russian. The local dialect is sufficiently different from the Armenian spoken in Yerevan that Armenian television uses subtitles when Karabakh villagers speak.

From Meghri in southern Armenia we went back up north through the mountains to Goris and then took a taxi to the Karabakh capital Stepanakert. At the border a sign in Armenian and French says "Welcome to Artsakh". Artsakh and Karabakh are interchangeable terms for the same place.

After arrival in Karabakh our law-abiding iPhones moved forward one hour to Azerbaijan time (GMT+5). In practice Karabakh operates on the same time as Armenia (GMT+4).

In Stepanakert, an official at the Ministry of Foreign Affairs, speaking polished English, gave us visas on the spot. These authorised us to visit all seven regions we had requested with the exception of the front line.

The next day, 21 September, we headed south by taxi on a quiet asphalt road to the town of Hadrut, the starting point of the trail. The driver dropped us by a church and we were on our own.

We had read the janapar.org website with information on the trail and digested some of its tips. Stock up with Imodium against diarrhoea, avoid both the powerful fruit vodka called *oghee* and romance with the locals. We heeded this advice but happily never needed the Imodium.

The one essential bit of kit is a GPS. With the assistance of janapar.org and the ViewRanger GPS app we downloaded everything we needed onto Tom's phone. We had a digital map of the trail, GPS guidance, written directions on the route and information on accommodation in each village at day's end. Much of the trail is waymarked with blue paint, but not all of it.

We walked up into the hills north of Hadrut and surveyed a pretty dry landscape, but much of the time we followed a shady tree-lined track with oaks and walnuts. It quickly became clear that the trail designers had worked with the need for shade in mind.

The first day was fairly gentle, sixteen kilometres, and on

arrival in our first village, Togh, we found accommodation with a butcher called Artur. His house was partly in ruins, but he was a good chef and for dinner he served up delicious pork shashlik garnished with pomegranate.

Artur sat with us for a while and we talked. He downed shots of *oghee* from a wooden cask sitting on the table and painted a gloomy picture of Togh. The population, he said, had dropped from about 10,000 a century ago, when Togh was a centre for the silk industry, to about 700 today. There are ruined buildings everywhere.

"There is no work. Life is hard," said Artur. I asked about the youth of Togh. What do they do? "They go to Russia," he said. "Stavropol, Volgograd."

He spoke disparagingly of Lenin and the 1917 Bolshevik Revolution and expressed nostalgia for the Russian Empire, of which Karabakh was a part. "When the tsars ruled it was better," he said.

But Togh is attempting a comeback, even without the tsars. In 2014 it held its first wine festival and in October 2015, he said, it would be inviting wine lovers to come back for more. Togh's red wine graces the menu of at least one top Yerevan restaurant.

On day two, heading for the village of Azokh, we walked through a sublime beech wood, still in the green garb of summer, but with a few leaves falling in a mesmeric slow-motion dance.

I think we looked tired on arrival. Two village women walked up to us separately and gave us grapes. We sat and feasted hungrily. We found accommodation in a house with a well-laden pomegranate tree and many hens and pigs. When I headed for the outdoor shower room one pig briefly joined me. This Karabakh trip is more a celebration of rural life than an ode to modern plumbing.

Day three and the landscape is arid. "It's a bit like *The Grapes of Wrath*" said Tom, invoking John Steinbeck's classic 1939 novel about farmers fleeing drought in Oklahoma. We had just walked past some abandoned farm machinery by the roadside in the village of Shekher. In Karabakh, rusting agricultural vehicles are a common sight.

At the end of day four we arrived in the village of Avetaranots. During these first four days we didn't see one bar or café. The standard of living is simply too low. Our routine on arrival in a village was to seek out a shop – there was always at least one – and buy the coldest beer they had.

In my memory these Karabakh villages quickly fused into one. I recall the hellos and the stares from neatly dressed school-children, the strutting geese, the grunting pigs and the kindness of strangers.

Our fifth day on the trail was a highlight. We were into our stride now and we bundled days five and six on the janapar.org site into a tough one-day hike to the old fortified town of Shushi which stands atop a cliff. After the village of Karintak the trail enters the dramatic Karkar Canyon. The path follows a river and is mainly a scramble through woodland, with a 700-metre high limestone wall visible through the trees.

Finally, a steep rocky path climbs to Shushi. Nothing can quite prepare you for this town, which is unlike anywhere I have ever seen. Soviet-era apartment blocks are not uplifting at the best of times. We entered Shushi along a dirt road with a forlorn inhabited block on our left and the empty shell of a ruined block, overgrown with weeds, to our right.

Twenty-one years after the end of the Karabakh war about half of Shushi still lies in ruins. But it is a functioning town, with about 5,000 inhabitants. During our visit there was a wedding in the white limestone cathedral. There are hotels, restaurants, cash dispensers, asphalted roads and four working museums.

Shushi, or Shusha to Azeris, has had a tortured history. In the early twentieth century it was one of the biggest towns of the South Caucasus, with a healthy economy based on silk manufacture, craftsmanship and trade.

With the benefit of hindsight, 1904 looks like a high water mark for multi-ethnic Shushi, which was important for both Christian Armenian and Muslim Azeri culture. In that year, Shakespeare's *Othello* was performed in Turkish in Shushi's 350-seat theatre. Things began to fall apart when Russia's 1905 revolution sent shockwaves through the empire. The events known to history as the Armenian-Tatar Massacres left many dead across the Caucasus. In Shushi hundreds were killed or wounded and the theatre was set on fire.

But fate reserved an even crueller blow for Shushi. In 1920 Azeri forces laid waste the Armenian quarter of the city, killing hundreds if not thousands. For the next forty years the Armenian quarter was a ghost town.

We stayed two nights in Shushi and had time to hear something of its more recent history. Saro Saryan, president of the Union for Armenian Refugees, gave us a guided tour of the history museum, with emphasis on the battle for Shushi in the Karabakh war.

Armenian forces captured the town in an extraordinary night attack on 8-9 May 1992. Two divisions with equipment strapped to their backs climbed the rock face on Shushi's southeast side. Azeri troops and Chechen volunteers led by Islamist commander Shamil Basayev fled. From then on the tide of war flowed in favour of the Armenians.

We sat for a while and talked in the small museum office. I asked Saro how he rated the risk of another Karabakh war. "Fifty-fifty," he said crisply. Saro offered advice to Europe. He is wary of Islam and he brought up the subject of migrants arriving in Europe, many from the Middle East. "You must be very careful with your prosperity," he said, counselling that European countries put limits on the number of migrants they would accept.

He depicted Christian Karabakh as a front line in a struggle against Islamic fundamentalism.

In Karabakh, the Azeri Muslim voices in the system are silent, because they were uprooted by war and left for Azerbaijan. Armenians, in their turn, were uprooted from Azerbaijan. Saro, for example, was born in Baku. As is usual in conflicts, each party feels aggrieved. This not an age-old conflict but a modern one. It is, however, a very bitter one.

As ever in war there are some gentle humanising touches. The trenches on the front line are in places only fifty metres apart and stories circulate that soldiers sometimes visit enemy trenches for a bit of a chinwag.

Time to clear our heads and move on. Day seven was a gentle stroll downhill to Stepanakert. This is a sort of Bonn of the Caucasus – a tranquil, provincial town catapulted into being a capital. It is true that small groups of soldiers wearing black berets can be seen of an evening, but perhaps the most striking thing about Stepanakert is how normal it looks and feels. The town is about thirty kilometres from the front line, but the mood seems relaxed and confident. There are no derelict buildings and some construction work is taking place.

Day eight and we walked to the village of Patara where we stayed in the home of Stepan Grigoryan and his mother, Emma. Unusually for Karabakh, Stepan speaks English. He works for the International Red Cross, partly helping land-mine victims to earn a living, and he also runs a small bread business with his mother.

Emma's kitchen buzzes with activity. She and a small team of women turn out 140 to 150 loaves of flat Armenian bread a day. The Karabakh war left Emma a widow and she brought up a young family alone. She used to be a post office worker and started the bread business one year ago.

Stepan joined us for dinner and suggested that I be the toastmaster. My first experience in the role of *tamada*! I was mindful that the main news reports in Karabakh were of a spate of violent deaths, eight in all, on or near the front line. I said we should follow the custom of the Georgian region of Adjara.

"The first toast is to peace," I said and we all raised our glasses of home-made blackberry wine.

Stepan was a much more cheerful drinking companion than Artur in the struggling town of Togh. He radiated youthful optimism and had already seen a bit of the world. He had been on a leadership course in France and combined an international perspective with a deep attachment to his country.

He expounded on the rule of Vachagan, who in the late fifth century and early sixth century AD built many churches, bridges and roads in Karabakh.

"Karabakh people say Karabakh is the centre of Armenia," said Stepan, whose flow was interrupted by one of the women walking in with a trayful of bread. He excused himself, since he had to pitch in and help. Before turning up at the Red Cross office, he does bread deliveries.

Day nine and the instruction on the janapar.org website is "Hike directly into the wilderness". It was without a doubt the toughest day of the trail, but very lovely. Some of the time there was no path. With GPS in hand we bushwhacked our way through pristine Karabakh forests, home to wolf, bear, lynx and jackal. We didn't actually see any of these creatures, but it bucked me tremendously to know that they were there. (On the previous evening, doubtless encouraged by the blackberry wine, during

As busy as it gets on the Janapar Trail

dinner I emitted quite a convincing wolf howl as we discussed our plans for the morrow.)

A particularly challenging part of the hike was a section around a spectacular natural rock called Kachaghakaberd, Fortress of the Magpies. Here local people took sanctuary in the eighth century from Arab invaders. This is a remote spot, with difficult terrain of sudden drops and thick bramble bushes. Without a GPS or local knowledge, heaven help you. Using the very last of our phone battery we reached the village of Kolatak where we spent the night.

Day ten and our journey's end. We arrived in the quirky mountain resort of Vank, which has its own little zoo, and checked into a hotel shaped like a ship. After a visit to the thirteenth-century monastery of Gandzasar, considered one of the masterpieces of Armenian architecture, we celebrated at a tiny timber-built restaurant by the roadside, with views over the wooded mountainsides.

We declined pig's head, but to the sound of a lion roaring we ate tasty vegetarian fare including Zhingalov hats, the Karabakh speciality of flatbread with a variety of herbs. We washed it down with local white wine. The walk was the longest that Tom or I had ever done and rarely have I enjoyed a meal so much.

We walked about 145 kilometres in all and never saw a single hiker on the trail, just the occasional man with donkey or horse. I found a lot to like about Karabakh. Tom's verdict? "I have to say, the hike has been a highlight of the year."

CHAPTER 13

The Armenian Genocide, 100 Years On

White carnations and red roses set the tone around the eternal flame at the Armenian Genocide memorial.

Atop a hill in Yerevan, the fire is inside a bowl surrounded by twelve slabs of basalt representing the provinces inside Turkey where Armenians lived before the mass killings perpetrated a century ago. In 1900 about two million Armenians lived in Turkey's eastern provinces. Twenty years later there was none – they either died violently or fled or were forcibly converted to Islam.

This memorial is redolent of loss. Mount Ararat, a national symbol for Armenians, dominates the view to the south. The mountain is on Turkish soil.

I have come here with participants in a conference on the Genocide. After they lay some flowers at the memorial we walk to the museum. Just outside is a small group of visitors led by a guide. He gestures towards Ararat and tells the group that only twenty kilometres away is the traditional homeland of Western Armenia, now part of Turkey.

In flawed but clearly understandable English, he tells the group, "Once it will be liberated again." This is not the view of the Armenian government, but his words still send a shiver right through me.

Emotions are raw in Armenia. Sometimes it can feel as if the killings happened only yesterday. Turkey, a NATO member, and Armenia, a Russian ally, are on glacial terms. The border between the two has been closed since 1993. Russian troops, stationed on Armenian soil, guard the frontier which is dotted with watchtowers.

The Armenian Genocide is a big, depressing subject. But in Yerevan, during this centennial year, it is a subject that cannot be avoided. Here is a summary of what happened and a look at why this story is still unfolding.

The official Armenian estimate of the number of Armenians killed in what was then the Ottoman Empire is 1.5 million. Some historians put the figure lower, in the range of 600,000 to one million.

The slaughter happened against the backdrop of the First World War, with fear swirling in the corridors of power in Istanbul that the empire faced the danger of oblivion. Ottoman troops fought on no fewer than nine fronts.

Even before the war the empire was in serious decline, having lost very extensive territories. In 1911, Italy made an unprovoked attack on the Turkish province of Libya. The two Balkan wars (1912-1913) then deprived the empire of nearly all its remaining territory in Europe. The wars forced more than 800,000 Muslims to flee eastwards as refugees.

Declining empires, it seems, sometimes go out not with a bang but a whimper. The Ottoman Empire, however, does not fit this mould. It went out with a boom that destroyed many lives.

In the First World War the Turks fought alongside Germany and Austria-Hungary. One of their enemies was the Russian Empire, which like Turkey had an Armenian population. After Russia suffered disastrous defeats on the eastern front in 1914, it had to pull troops away from the Caucasus front with Turkey.

Russia then actively recruited volunteers, including Armenians, to bolster its army in the Caucasus. The Russians, with ethnic Armenian soldiers in their ranks, proceeded to inflict a most terrible defeat on the Ottoman Third Army at the battle of Sarikamish, at the end of 1914 and the beginning of 1915. Enver Pasha, one of the 'Three Pashas' leading Turkey, blamed the Armenians for the bloodbath and the stage was set for Turkey's revenge.

But much needs to be added to this barest of outlines. Armenians suffered in a whole series of massacres in the Ottoman Empire before 1915. There were killings in 1894, 1895, 1896 and 1909.

Nor were these small-scale affairs. The bloodletting of the mid-1890s, generally referred to as the Hamidian massacres, resulted in the deaths of between 100,000 and 300,000 Armenians. Most of the slaughter was carried out by government troops often supported by crowds.

There are themes present in the violence against Armenians which have echoes in later twentieth-century genocides. Armenians tended to be better off than the Turks. Many were merchants or industrialists while Turks were often peasant farmers or low-paid functionaries. 'The Jews of the Orient' is a label that has sometimes been pinned on the Armenians.

Historian Ronald Grigor Suny, in *They Can Live in the Desert but Nowhere Else,* A History of the Armenian Genocide, highlights competition for land as one factor behind anti-Armenian feeling. In the Rwanda genocide, land hunger was also an issue.

Tensions over land between Armenians and Kurds had simmered for decades in eastern Anatolia before any of the mass killings happened.

Kurds carried out much of the slaughter in the Genocide. Now, a century later, with Armenians gone from eastern Turkey, the tensions in this part of the world directly pit Kurds against Turks.

Back to 1915. The museum in Yerevan sets out a tragedy in three acts. The first act was the extermination of Armenian soldiers serving in the Ottoman army. The second act was the murder of business, political and cultural leaders. The final sickening act was the deportations to the deserts of Syria.

This has to be one of the truly terrible images of the twentieth century. Straggling lines of Armenians, many of them women and children, made the nightmare journey on foot to the desert. If they weren't shot, abducted or starved en route they died on arrival at concentration camps.

One notorious camp was Meskene on the Euphrates river. Typhus, cholera and hunger claimed many lives. There was also deliberate killing.

The museum says of the camp: "Armenians were burned with oil, asphyxiated with wet wood smoke and blown up with explosives. The number of Armenians killed in Meskene during the Genocide is estimated to be 100,000."

Not all Armenians were deported and in many places they perished in barbaric ways. In the city of Diyarbakir, ruled by an ardent Turkish nationalist, Dr Mehmed Reşid, some had red-hot horseshoes driven through their bodies. Diyarbakir's bishop was doused with petrol and set on fire in front of a crowd. The flames were extinguished before he met death and he was thrown into a stable where an American missionary found him dying in great pain. Dr Reşid ordered hundreds of Armenian children to be thrown to their deaths from an arched bridge just outside the city.

Further east, closer to Lake Van, there was also terrible slaughter. One Turk, Vehib Paşa, who was to become commander of the Ottoman Third Army, spoke of "atrocity of a kind never before seen in the history of Islam".

At the time of the massacres, the world did sit up and take

notice. In May 1915 the governments of Britain, France and Russia put out a joint statement denouncing the "crimes of Turkey against humanity and civilisation" and calling Turkey to account. It was the first time an international text had used such words.

The media covered the atrocities. The *New York Times*, by one count, carried 145 articles in 1915 alone.

But killings resumed in 1920-1923 and the world seemed to forget about the Armenians. In the museum there is a chilling quote from Adolf Hitler, who said in 1939, "Who, after all, speaks today of the annihilation of the Armenians?"

Suny writes that "little distanced reflection or scholarly attention was paid to the massacres of the Armenians and Assyrians for almost fifty years after the events."

In other words, the killings did not really sink deep into world memory for a very long time. I discussed all of this with a German writer, Heide Rieck, whom I met in Yerevan.

Heide, a grey-haired woman in her mid-seventies, first heard about the massacres from a Turk in eastern Turkey thirty years ago. He told her how very cruel it had all been. She has since made it her business to publicise the Armenian cause in her native land. Back in 1915, Germany made no attempt to restrain its ally Turkey from shedding Armenian blood.

I asked Heide why, in her view, the world paid so little attention for so long to the scale of the atrocities. She pondered this and suggested that the emigration of many surviving Armenians after the Genocide to Western Europe and North America had meant that individual Armenians spent a lot of energy just adjusting to new homelands. They had little appetite for spreading word about the calamity which had befallen their nation.

There was another factor at play – the ability of the Turkish authorities to apply diplomatic pressure abroad to leave the subject alone. In 1933, writer Franz Werfel, an Austrian Jew, published his epic novel *The Forty Days of Musa Dagh* about the heroic resistance of an Armenian village during the Genocide. When MGM Studios decided to film the story, the Turkish government had a word with the US State Department and the project died.

Ripples from the atrocity keep spreading and have now reached distant corners of the world. In 2015, a statue commemorating the Genocide was set up at St Davids cathedral in the southwest corner of Wales. The statue, depicting the Virgin Mary, a Christ child and a replica of an Armenian church, adorn a lawn in the cloisters. Some years ago, one of the cathedral's canons visited Armenia and his interest in the tragedy kindled awareness in that corner of Europe.

Successive Turkish governments have not been apologetic about the wholesale slaughter. The official Turkish view of events is that the deaths occurred during a civil war in which both Armenians and Turks died. The Turkish government vehemently rejects the position taken by Armenia that this was genocide.

Some endorse the Turkish view that this was not genocide and point to the fact that the Turks, unlike the Nazis with their persecution of the Jews, made no attempt to pursue their victims beyond the boundaries of the state.

But although there is not complete consensus, there has been a discernible shift, with more scholars, spiritual leaders and governments backing the view that genocide is the correct term.

Suny, in his book, stresses that there was a centralised chain of command that began in the Ottoman capital, Istanbul. Talat Paşa, the minister of the interior, was the main man directing the carnage from afar. He had a private telegraph in his home and at night he sent orders to his henchmen.

Six years after the Genocide, in March 1921, an Armenian

revolutionary shot Talat dead with a single bullet when he came out of his house in Berlin.

In this, the centenary year, the world has been paying some attention.

In April 2015, Pope Francis said at a mass in the Armenian Catholic rite at St. Peter's Basilica that humanity had lived through three massive tragedies over the past century.

"The first, which is widely considered 'the first genocide of the twentieth century', struck your own Armenian people," he said, naming the other two as the crimes committed by Nazism and Stalinism. "Concealing or denying evil is like allowing a wound to keep bleeding without bandaging it," said the pope.

An angry Turkey promptly recalled its envoy to the Vatican.

Several of the world's most powerful governments, including the United States and Germany, have not backed the view that it was genocide.

In Yerevan, I met people who have engaged with the issue because they feel more needs to be done to redress the wrongs done. Heide Rieck, the German author, was the one I talked to most.

Undaunted by her lack of knowledge of Armenian, Heide worked with a colleague to publish a book of Armenian verse in German translation. The book, entitled *Und sticht in meine Seele* (And it stings in my soul), contains poetry by Paruyr Sevak (1924-1971), one of Armenia's best-loved modern poets.

I asked about the themes of Sevak's poetry. "The main theme is love," said Heide, adding that Sevak's death in a car accident had been widely blamed on the KGB since he was critical of Soviet corruption. She said she was in Armenia this time partly to plant some trees for a garden to nurture Armenian-German friendship.

Heide told me about a conference and we walked together to the National Academy of Sciences of Armenia, venue of an international gathering with the title *Armenian Genocide – 100, From Recognition to Reparation*. I went in and was made welcome.

It was a conference of more than 100 academics from Armenia, Russia, Europe, Australia and North America. They looked at a wide range of topics, including the impact of the Genocide on the arts, but the meatiest, most newsy issue was reparations from Turkey.

A lecturer in general education from the American University of Armenia, David Davidian, told the conference that he estimated the material losses of Armenians in the Genocide at three trillion dollars. This did not take into account any compensation for loss of life or injury.

One participant, Armen Marukyan, gave me a copy of his book *The Basis and Opportunities of Applying to International Court on the case of the Armenian Genocide*. It goes into legalities in some detail. Marukyan writes that before the Genocide, Armenians in eastern Turkey had 1,860 churches and chapels, 451 monasteries and about 2,000 schools.

The conference had the usual formality of academia, but it also felt quite cosy. The community of genocide specialists is fairly small. At the end a portly Russian professor with a red bow tie and matching handkerchief in his jacket pocket, Vladimir Sakharov, grandly handed out medals. Have we suddenly been taken in a time machine back to the Soviet era, I wondered.

The conference decided not to make any formal announcement to the media about its proceedings. I think conversation among academics about reparations from Turkey will trundle on for a while before they take any advice to the government, which has not so far brought a legal case against Turkey. From 1920 to 1991 Armenia was part of the Soviet Union and was not in a position to bring a lawsuit.

At conference close we all climbed into a bus and headed off to the Armenian Genocide memorial to lay flowers. Just below the centre is one of many billboards in the city commemorating the centenary. Its message reads, "I remember and demand".

No one who has studied the chilling events of 1915 in Anatolia can doubt the scale of the atrocities. Without spelling out the obvious on this billboard, what Armenia demands is that Turkey's government also remembers and apologises for what happened during those fearful months a century ago.

Turkey applied for membership of what is now the European Union back in 1987. The fact that it is still drumming its fingers in the waiting room to the EU, two decades later, stems partly from its amnesia over the Genocide.

The late British historian Tony Judt, in the epilogue to his book *Postwar A History of Europe since 1945*, has much to say on the subject of genocides and remembering. He argues that in the twenty-first century a core part of Europe's identity is that it did remember, it did come terms with the Holocaust, the Nazi genocide of the Jews.

The long march of time will ultimately blot out most memories of atrocities, but Judt puts his finger on a key point when he writes, "A nation has first to have remembered something before it can begin to forget it."

CHAPTER 14

Armenia, the First Christian Nation

If people know just one thing about Armenia, they know that this was the first Christian nation.

The traditionally accepted date of Armenia's adoption of Christianity as state religion is 301 AD. It is a big part of Armenia's self-image that this country led the way in the official acceptance of Christ's teachings.

In recent years some scholars have made a tentative case for Ethiopia having precedence – they have cast doubt over the accuracy of the Armenian date of 301. It would probably make some Armenians cross if scholarly opinion ever conclusively deprived them of the title of first Christian state.

But there's a question that interests me more than who came first. It is this: how was Christianity spread in the early centuries? After arriving in Armenia I realised with a start that I knew little about the first centuries of the world's largest religion.

I chiefly had in my head the image of the early Christian as martyr, cruelly fed to the lions by the Romans. But in Armenia I was suddenly confronted with the image of early Christian as warrior, waging a religious war against pagans.

One secondary source on Armenia's history is Yuri Babayan's English-language website armenianhistory.info.

He writes that King Tiridates, having converted to Christianity, "implanted the new religion with fire and sword. The sanctuaries and heathen temples were destroyed throughout the country. The only pagan temple remained intact to this day is Garni."

Now there is nothing in the Sermon on the Mount, of course, about the need to smite the heathen with fire and sword. This bloodletting happened seventeen centuries ago, but still I find it more than a little disappointing. It is surely not what Jesus Christ had in mind. King Tiridates had, in theory, accepted a gospel of love.

I went to the temple at Garni, on a day trip out of Yerevan. It was a welcome change from the big city. In a taxi we drove along nearly empty roads up into the mountains. The sun shone, the trees were in their autumn colours and the great white majesty of Ararat dominated the view off to the southwest.

Garni was built on the edge of a cliff in the second half of the first century AD and is mentioned in the Annals of Tacitus. It is the only Greco-Roman style building anywhere in the former Soviet Union. Dedicated to the sun god Mihr, it was built by an Armenian king following rules of sacred geometry. The most sacred numbers were three, six and nine, the last being the holiest number of them all.

Today Garni is one of Armenia's most popular tourist attractions. What visitors see is essentially a reconstruction, completed in the mid-1970s. The temple is also the main shrine for a small number of neo-pagans, who tap into Armenia's pre-Christian beliefs which King Tiridates did not root out. They come here for ceremonies, particularly on 21 March, the pagan New Year.

From Garni we drove on a few kilometres to one of Christianity's most sacred sites in Armenia, Geghard monastery. This is a place of great beauty and tranquillity. In the summer months many visitors come but in October it retained the feel of a sanctuary, a retreat.

Geghard, the Monastery of the Holy Lance, stands near the head of a valley with tall cliffs on three sides. It has been a site of Christian worship since the fourth century when St Gregory the Illuminator, who converted King Tiridates to Christianity, founded a monastery complex here. Some churches within the complex are dug out of the cliff face.

The monastery gets its name from the fact that for centuries it kept the lance which Christians believed pierced the side of Jesus when he was nailed on the cross.

Geghard monastery is emphatic that it has the genuine article. According to a sign for visitors: "Other spears lay claim to being the true spear, including ones in Vienna, Kraków and Rome but the Geghard spear is celebrated in Armenia as the one True Lance."

The day before my pilgrimage to Geghard monastery I went to Echmiadzin, about twenty kilometres to the west of Yerevan. This is Armenia's Vatican and it was the capital of the country when Christianity became the state religion.

According to tradition, St Gregory was divinely guided to build the first Mother Church of Armenia (Mayr Tachar) in Echmiadzin on the spot where a beam of light fell. Building took place in 301-303. The original structure fell into ruin and successive building took place at later periods, but Echmiadzin cathedral is considered the oldest in the world. When I visited it was having a bit of a facelift.

In its treasury is the Holy Lance, set in a gold and silver casing, which was once at Geghard. The treasury also has what it describes as fragments of Noah's Ark. According to the Book of Genesis, Noah's Ark came to rest on a mountain in the Ararat range, which is clearly visible from Echmiadzin. Armenians consider themselves to be direct descendants of Noah.

I travelled to Echmiadzin on a Sunday and the city was buzzing with life. At the Surp Gayane church a succession of weddings was taking place. Just outside the church were several violinists and a white Rolls-Royce.

So where do Armenia's posh neo-pagan weddings happen? At Garni temple, of course.

On a long journey the traveller has a mix of companions. Some are real flesh-and-blood human beings, while others can be writers who have already passed this way and given us their impressions.

In my musings on Armenian Christianity one boon companion has been Vasily Grossman, Russian war correspondent and novelist extraordinaire. I wonder whether any journalist past or present could equal his gift for just being there, in the maelstrom, at the moment that history was being made.

For five months Grossman covered the Battle of Stalingrad, that epic turning point in the Second World War. He covered Kursk, the biggest tank battle in history. He was there, in Berlin, when the Third Reich finally fell and he visited Hitler's office. Grossman, a Jew, went to Treblinka and gave one of the first eyewitness accounts of a Nazi death camp.

Out of his experiences came his great war novel *Life and Fate*, which gives the feel of Russia after Hitler's Operation Barbarossa plunged the Soviet Union into a life-or-death war. Grossman has an eye for the image that lingers in the mind. He describes Lady Cripps, wife of the British ambassador, eating supper in a hotel restaurant in exchange for a meal coupon. She wraps leftover bread and sugar lumps in newspaper and takes them to her room.

KGB agents confiscated the manuscript of *Life and Fate* – the novel highlights similarities between Nazism and Communism – and notoriously even took Grossman's carbon paper and typing ribbons. Not knowing whether his novel would ever see the light of day, Grossman went off to Armenia on a translation assignment. Out of this journey, undertaken in 1961, came *An Armenian Sketchbook*.

It is a work suffused with such tenderness that it often feels like a love song and in the closing lines Grossman says that he wrote it with love. I read the book after I had left the Caucasus and while I was digesting what I had seen, but what Grossman says about religion in Armenia struck me with all the force of truth. His sense was that Armenia, in its soul, was not Christian but pagan.

"Nowhere – neither in town nor village – did I see any believers; what I saw were people carrying out rites. You don't hear or see a believer; you sense them. In Armenia I did not once sense a believer. I saw many old men and women in the villages – and I never sensed the presence of faith in them."

Grossman wrote that what he found was the spirit of paganism. "I sensed it in the way the Armenians drink wine, eat meat, bake bread and perform rites. I sensed it in the way they walk, sing and laugh. I did not sense the spirit of Christianity, even though Armenian churches still look splendid while their pagan temples are all in ruins."

I am sure that Grossman, a Jew, did not write these words in a spirit of criticism. He loved Armenians. They had suffered like the Jews had suffered.

But I concur with his opinion that the spirit of Armenia is pagan. Vahagn, the ancient pre-Christian god of war and courage, is a popular given name in Armenia even today.

CHAPTER 15

A Pythonesque Armenian

In Yerevan, I have been on a bit of a cultural bender. For starters, I went to the city's Stanislavsky Russian Theatre to see жизнь не сыграешь на бис (Life doesn't play an encore), a medley of Russian music and poetry. It drew on the work of several twentieth-century geniuses, including actor-singer Vladimir Vysotsky, a favourite of mine, and poet Marina Tsvetaeva.

It must be intimidating for actors when they work in a theatre named after the great Konstantin Stanislavsky, whose plea to actors was "keep breaking traditions, I beg you".

But this troupe from Moscow was spirited and professional, serving up entertainment that had pace and depth. Two actors came among the audience and daintily handed out little bunches of grapes. It was a nice touch. After all, the autumn is grape harvest time and this is the Caucasus, with its traditions of hospitality.

The next day the German writer Heide Rieck suggested an outing to the museum in Yerevan dedicated to the work of Sergei Parajanov, Armenian filmmaker and artist. I am always happy to be educated, so off we went.

The museum is housed in a traditional two-storey Caucasus building. Small museums, if they have charm, are important in the overall cultural scheme of things. And the Sergei Parajanov Museum does have charm.

Parajanov (1924-1990) was a playful iconoclast who had the misfortune to ply his trade as Surrealist artist during the time of the Soviet Union, not an entity known for its sense of fun and its tolerance of artistic innovation.

The museum has on display more than 1,000 exhibits, including dolls, collages, sculptures and artworks which Parajanov produced while languishing in a Soviet prison camp. The visitor can also watch sequences from his most famous film, *The Color of Pomegranates*, made in 1969.

In photographs, the artist stares out at us with a handsome, unsmiling face. He looks strong, almost fierce, and he sports a dark trimmed beard, moustache and bushy eyebrows. He looks sharp – good company if you have got your mind in gear, rather intimidating if you don't.

So why do I call him a Pythonesque Armenian? Well, his collages can look as if they have come straight out of *Monty Python's Flying Circus*. As soon as I saw the collage he did in 1987 called *Death of my Sister Ruzanna* I immediately thought: Monty Python.

Then I read one film critic who said that when he watched *The Color of Pomegranates* he thought of Monty Python sketches sending up ever so intellectual art films. I know what he meant – there are intense brooding silences.

At the same time, I would not want to rubbish the film. It has sequences that I find spellbindingly beautiful. *Time Out Film Guide* included Parajanov's masterpiece in its list of Top 100 Films. It will surely endure for as long as people watch films.

The first version of *The Color of Pomegranates* was called *Sayat Nova* (The King of Song) and it is partly based on the life of the eighteenth-century Armenian poet of that name. But it is not a conventional biography. Sayat Nova's life serves as the framework for tableaux vivants drawn from the religious and artistic life of his country.

Pomegranates spill their juice forming the shape of a map of old Armenia. The pages of many open books turn in the breeze. A woman dances to the sound of drums in front of great hanging carpets.

Art films are not meant to be minutely dissected. If you have never seen *The Color of Pomegranates*, it is on YouTube. I find it visually stunning.

The Soviet authorities, unfortunately, did not appreciate Parajanov's work. From 1973 to 1977 he was in a Soviet prison camp and for years he was effectively prevented from film-making. His collages and other art forms were a sort of creative release because he couldn't make films.

Before writing these words I looked at my theatre programme to learn the name of the theatre company which had provided the excellent evening of Russian music and poetry.

There are no prizes for guessing this. I discovered that it was the Parajanov Moscow Art Theatre. I think the artist would have liked the show, including the Armenian grapes.

CHAPTER 16

Armenia's Independence Generation

Davit Dilanyan was born in 1991, the year the Soviet Union collapsed and Armenia threw off Moscow rule after seventy-one years. That makes Davit a member of what Armenians call the independence generation, the young people who have grown up in an independent state.

I met Davit, a professional facilitator, when he was running a workshop at the hostel in Yerevan where I was staying. On a day after the workshop ended, we went for a leisurely coffee and talked about life, the universe and everything Armenian.

Davit is slightly built, gentle, alert and full of nervous energy. He is patriotic, steeped in his country's difficult history yet forward-looking. Our conversation ranged widely, from the emergence of a pub culture in Yerevan to Armenians' backing for President Bashar al-Assad of war-shattered Syria.

First I asked David about his youth. His early years coincided with a period of extraordinary challenge, when Armenia fell back to a pre-industrial way of life. War with Azerbaijan over Nagorno-Karabakh and the dissolution of the Soviet Union meant Armenia had scant electricity.

Davit grew up in a small town near Yerevan. He has memories of universal poverty, very little light and his brother heading off to collect firewood to keep the home fires burning.

"I remember them grey and dark actually these years. But I always remember candles," he said. He recalled his mother rushing to do household chores like washing during the one or two hours of daily electricity.

"But actually people were happier in a way then," he said. "Because the neighbourhood was amazing. I remember visiting each other and, yeah, we had really nice neighbours… I think in a way that society was equal then. There was not much 'rich people or poor people'. They were all poor."

"We don't have the best economic situation," said Davit. "It's probably the worst in the South Caucasus." Electricity shortages are a thing of the past, but Armenia has low wages and few exports, mainly brandy, wine, fresh fruit and minerals. Its borders with Turkey and Azerbaijan are closed so it relies on road links with Georgia to the north and Iran to the south.

I asked Davit what was working well in Armenia and that moved us into a whole discussion of the independence generation. He said many young Armenians were getting a good education and often spoke several languages.

It was the young, he said, who had taken the lead in street protests in June 2015 over a planned increase in electricity prices. These protests lasted more than ten days and made international headlines. They were a challenge for the Armenian government because the distribution firm planning the hike was a subsidiary of a Russian company and Russia is a key ally. The protesters basically won the day.

Davit painted a picture of Yerevan youth leading the way and older people then joining the ranks of protesters.

"I think all of Yerevan stood next to these young people," said Davit. "They got really inspired."

He said the country was benefiting from the non-conformist stance taken by Armenia's pro-independence and environmental movements back in the late 1980s.

"The people who stood up then taught their children not to be conformist. The independence generation is really active. This is the future of Armenia, I am sure," said Davit. "For example, the pub life comes from our generation. I am sure there was nothing like that seven or eight years ago."

He described pub life as the symbol of the youth of Armenia. "I don't think the pubs are places for getting drunk in Armenia," said Davit. "You just go there to hang out and to have a nice time." Often there was music and you could dance. There were rock pubs. Members of NGOs, entrepreneurs often gathered in pubs to discuss plans.

Davit approved of the spread of pubs in Yerevan, but he disapproved of one associated development. "Girls started to smoke a lot in Armenia. It is a bad trend for me."

When I asked Davit what was not working well, he said there was corruption and nepotism in Armenia, but less than there had been a decade or so ago. In no time at all the conversation focused on emigration.

"For me this is the biggest problem," said Davit. "I don't like to judge people, but I feel if they tried harder they could stay."

He knows from firsthand experience that the economic pull drawing people away from Armenia can be very strong. He studied in an Erasmus programme in Italy for seven months and received a grant of 1,000 euros a month. Back in Armenia studying for a PhD he gets a grant of between forty and fifty euros a month. Nor is money the only reason that emigration appears attractive to some. Young Armenian men are expected to serve two years in the army. Davit said the continuing conflict with Azerbaijan over

Karabakh was one factor behind emigration "because there are still shootings and deaths alongside the border".

He immediately said that he was getting very stressed when he read news reports about Islamic State.

"My first message is peace for all the world," he said.

Then our conversation took a turn which surprised me. Making his plea for peace, Davit had tapped into the deepest, most terrible memories of his race. Since the Genocide, Armenians see the world through the prism of who stood by them in their hour of need. Davit told me that Syrians had been the first people to offer sanctuary to Armenians fleeing from the massacres in the Ottoman Empire.

He said Armenians still felt gratitude to Syria and he praised Assad for what he felt was the Syrian president's supportive policy towards religious minorities.

"Armenians are rather in favour of Assad," said Davit, whose plea for world peace just minutes earlier had come across as totally heartfelt.

One strong impression I have after talking to Davit is that Armenia is a bridge country between East and West. Davit is fluent in Armenian, Russian and English. He is writing his PhD on the Eurasian Economic Union, the political and economic bloc set up by Russia and to which Armenia belongs. Davit's girlfriend is Czech and lives in Prague where Davit is a fairly frequent visitor.

We need bridge countries and bridge people, even if some of their views do not accord with our own.

CHAPTER 17

Gyumri

"When sorrows come, they come not single spies, but in battalions."

These words from *Hamlet* are well-worn, but they are tragically apposite for Armenia's second city, Gyumri.

The sorrows began when an earthquake devastated the city in 1988 and then continued with the collapse of the Soviet Union three years later. This epic unravelling of the world's biggest state gutted all industry in Gyumri that had survived the natural disaster.

Over the last generation, few cities surely have contended with such challenges. I travelled north from Yerevan, through a barren, stony landscape, to see how Gyumri was faring today.

What I found was a complex story of decline, poverty and hope. The poverty is more shocking than I had expected, but the signs of hope are real.

I'll let Armenians tell the story of that first hammer blow. This is from a text in Armenian and Russian on a commemorative plaque outside a central church:

"At 11:41 on December 7, on a misty and bleak December day in 1988, the mountains gave a start and with great force shook the earth.

"Towns, villages, schools, nurseries and industrial plants were instantly destroyed and more than one million people were left homeless.

"At this tragic hour, 25,000 people died, 140,000 were injured and 16,000 were rescued from the rubble."

Big events like Armenia's earthquake rupture time. When the people of Gyumri talk about their lives, they often say that something happened "before the earthquake" or "after the earthquake". The point is that lives dramatically changed. There really was a before and an after. Even if your house was still standing, even if your whole family survived, you emerged into a changed world.

In Gyumri, I went to a bed and breakfast run by Artush and Raisa Davtyan. Artush told me that they had been at home with their two sons watching a Russian film on television when the earthquake struck. He remembers the floor of their stone-built house rising about half a metre as the shockwaves rippled through the building. Everyone in the family emerged unscathed and amazingly the house withstood the ordeal.

Before the earthquake Artush, now a tourist guide, was a scientist working in the physics department of a research institute. But the disaster knocked the stuffing out of Armenia's finances and after the earthquake there was no research work for Artush or his colleagues.

"Many people, they lost their jobs," said Artush. "We had to work anywhere. I became as a common worker. I worked in the building companies. I was in Russia, I worked in Russia later and I came back. I started to work here to rebuild our city and I worked in foreign building companies and step by step, later, I worked in a hotel."

Artush said that in the immediate aftermath of the quake Moscow promised a rapid rebuilding of Gyumri, along the lines of the heroic resurrection of Tashkent in Central Asia after its tremor in 1966. But times had changed and the Soviet Union was in terminal decline as a state. There was no repeat performance of fraternal workers arriving from other Soviet republics to rebuild a shattered city.

After the Soviet Union ceased to be, supply lines between the republics collapsed and there was a further giddy shrinking of the city's economy.

Artush said that Gyumri's textile factory had been the second biggest in the Soviet Union, employing 10,000 workers, mainly women. But with the end of the Soviet Union the supply of cotton from Uzbekistan stopped and the factory closed. He said a buyer of the plant carted all the machinery off to the Iranian city of Shiraz.

Today, most of Gyumri has finally been rebuilt. But work is scarce, wages are low and people are leaving in search of a better life. Studies have shown that nowhere in Armenia is depopulation so severe.

"Entire families just lock their doors and off they go to Russia," said Artush's wife Raisa. "The city is crumbling."

Journeys by taxi turn into a running commentary from the driver on how the city is declining. On one taxi ride through Gyumri, the driver pointed to the left side of the street and said to me, "That was an institute – closed." Then on our right, "All those shops – closed." Back on the left, "That was a dairy – closed."

I went to see the mayor, Samvel Balasanyan, to get his take on matters. The mayor, a tall, broad-shouldered man who is one of Armenia's leading beer magnates, told me in his office that the population of Gyumri had dropped from 225,000 at the time of the earthquake to 125,000 today.

He struck a philosophical note. "It is not like everyone leaves and forgets the city," he said. "There are a lot of people going and coming back. And the other thing about people leaving is that life is going at its natural pace. If people have bad housing conditions or can't find jobs it is very natural for them to leave."

The mayor said that 2,500 families still lived in metal containers put up after the earthquake as temporary accommodation. He refused to be drawn on when the last of these families would finally get proper homes, saying it depended on finance.

Did he expect the exodus from Gyumri to stop at some point? "Yes, of course it will."

During the interview, a city hall official named Armen Hovsepyan acted as my interpreter. It turned out that Armen was one of the unfortunates who still lived in a metal container. Indeed, except for four years when he studied in Utah he had lived in this 'temporary dwelling' since he was a baby. He said these containers were designed to last as homes for four years and they were poor protection against the elements.

"When it rains outside, it rains inside," he said. "It is crazy cold in the winter."

The day after my conversation with the mayor, Armen took me to see his home. Technically, it is two metal containers placed side by side. There is a sitting-out area by the front door, a living room, one bedroom and the kitchen. In the ceiling above the kitchen table a tear is clearly visible in the fabric. Armen shares this home with his mother and an elderly female friend of the family.

All around their house the urban landscape is an endless succession of metal containers still housing people.

At the time of the earthquake Armen was a four-month-old baby, living with his mother in a third floor apartment just metres from where he lives now. He is lucky to be alive. Rescuers got to him probably just in the nick of time.

"It took seven hours to get me out of the apartment, in freezing cold," he said.

Although Armen has an American university degree, fluent English and a responsible job in city hall's department of foreign affairs and tourism, his monthly salary is just 50,000 drams ($104).

I never asked Armen outright why he had come back, but I didn't really need to. He has such an obvious love for his city. For me, extended travel only makes sense when you meet people like Armen, who love their patch of the earth. The fact that he was in Gyumri at all struck me as being part of the hope for the city.

One of the hats that Armen wears is as a volunteer at a charitable foundation, which is trying to raise funds to make Gyumri a better place and persuade people to stay. The foundation website is www.gyumriprojecthope.org.

At city hall, his main job now is to attract tourists and I doubt that Gyumri could find a better person to do this. Armen knows his city well and conversation about it just comes tumbling out of him.

Did I know, he asked, that Gyumri's nineteenth-century Church of the Holy Saviour, still being rebuilt after the quake, was a copy of the cathedral in Ani, the ruined Armenian city over the border in Turkey?

"The architect went every Thursday by horse and carriage to copy the details of the cathedral," said Armen.

Ani, which thrived in the Middle Ages, is an enduring source of fascination for Armenians. The fact that, like Mount Ararat, it is on Turkish soil feels deeply wrong to them.

"Ani and Armenia are connected with underground tunnels," said Armen. "My uncle knows one of the entrances."

It was Armen who told me that Gyumri was the birthplace of George Ivanovich Gurdjieff, a twentieth-century mystic and spiritual teacher who still has a following. Gurdjieff was an early example of a modern thinker who sought to take the wisdom of the East to the West. It seems absolutely right that he was from Gyumri, an Armenian Christian city with Kurdish Yazidi villages in the surrounding area.

There is a school of thought that Gurdjieff was a charlatan, but then the same could probably be said of many a spiritual teacher. He certainly attracted some interesting followers, including a senior officer in British military intelligence and a Harley Street psychiatrist.

With his shaven head, black moustache and piercing eyes, Gurdjieff was a striking figure even in the world of esoteric thought. His father, a cattle herdsman and bardic poet, is buried in Gyumri and Armen told me that some Americans come to the city solely on account of the Gurdjieff link.

Today Gurdjieff's most widely read book is *Meetings with Remarkable Men,* available as a Penguin Modern Classic. It is a strange, compelling work, written by a man who seems totally larger than life. Who knows what is fact and what is fiction in it? Much of it is given over to accounts of his travels in search of spiritual truth. It builds up to a surreal tale of travelling to look for a legendary city in the waterless Gobi Desert with companions who first spend a month separately mulling ideas on how to tackle this journey. They decide to travel with stilts. These can serve the dual purpose of enabling them to stand tall and see above sandstorms, or they can be hitched to sheep so that the travellers can proceed in style on litters. This presumably is a fictional teaching story and the reader is invited to extract some deep meaning.

A recurring theme is Gurdjieff's colourful approach to earning money. Generally speaking he acted ethically, whether he was shining shoes in Rome or diving for coins thrown by steamboat passengers in the Bosphorus. But not always. In his youth, he tells us, he helped to survey the route for a planned railway in the South

Caucasus. He says that besides his official pay he received income "of a rather questionable character".

"Knowing beforehand which villages and little towns the railway was to go past, I would send someone to the power-possessors of these villages and towns, offering to 'arrange' for the railway to be laid through these places."

Later, in Samarkand, he dyes sparrows and sells them to locals as a rare kind of American canary, making sure that he leaves before there is any risk of rain. I am highlighting one aspect of a complex man and, paradoxically, the book is suffused with a strong sense of human brotherhood. In Gyumri, Turks killed his father, an ethnic Greek. Gurdjieff tells us this, but nowhere in the book does he speak ill of the Turks.

For those with no interest whatsoever in Gurdjieff, does Gyumri make sense as a holiday destination?

I would certainly say it makes sense as part of an Armenian tour. If you stay in a cosy B&B, as I did, there is no shortage of creature comforts.

The city is not rich, but it has a welcoming feel, smart people and a bustling market. Step nimbly past the ageing Ladas driving by and you enter an outdoor market that is just as I like them. In my book, markets should be noisy and this one is. There is the whirr of coffee grinders and the banging of metal in shops selling wood stoves – you can feel the ancient lineage of this place.

This being Armenia, the fare on offer in late October included grapes, grapes and more grapes, nuts of all kinds, live fish, crayfish, Armenian cognac, pomegranate wine, spices, coffees, carpets and Turkish electric heaters.

I want to open up one final new thread, to give more substance to my assertion that there are real signs of hope in Gyumri. I went one day to see the work of a foundation financed by diaspora money. The Tumo Center for Creative Technology, funded by the US-based Simonian Educational Foundation, opened a branch in Gyumri in September 2015. It is doing impressive things with youngsters between the ages of twelve and eighteen.

They come after school, typically for two workshops a week, and can choose free courses from the four areas of animation, film-making, computer game development and web design.

When I dropped by, there were dozens of youngsters in the classroom and spanking new Apple computers everywhere. The manager who briefed me at Tumo was a feisty young woman who grew up in Los Angeles, Nare Avagyan.

After hearing so much in Armenia about emigration, it was a most refreshing change to meet a sparky young Californian who had come home to her Armenian roots. Nare has been living in Armenia since 2012.

The Tumo Center struck me as a good example of the American 'can do' philosophy, allied to Armenian patriotism and Armenian-American money – all in all, a potent mix.

Nare said of the centre, "This is huge because Tumo really changes a generation, because kids start young and they are exposed to so much that it really helps them unlock their creative potential."

"All they need is motivation and a longing for learning and our doors are open to them, so any kid can come, register and take part."

In Yerevan the Tumo Center has more than 6,000 active students, she said.

"In Gyumri we are at full capacity, near 1,000 students," said Nare. "We also have over 500 kids on the wait list and, of course, we are going to do everything to accommodate them."

The Tumo Center in Gyumri is in temporary accommodation

CHAPTER 18

In Two Minds about Abkhazia

The world, it seems, is in two minds about Abkhazia, a Black Sea statelet at the western end of Georgia.

For Russians, it is a subtropical holiday paradise and they go there literally by the million every year. For the governments of the West, on the other hand, it is a dangerous no-go zone and they advise their citizens not to set foot in these badlands.

In 2015 I went three times to the South Caucasus and made it to quite a few places, but back home in Wales it gnawed at me that I had not set foot in Abkhazia. This felt like a serious omission and I decided to find out who is right about Abkhazia – the Russians or the West.

In international law this lush, beautiful region is part of Georgia, but covert Russian forces played their part in wresting it from Georgia in a war fought by Abkhaz nationalists in the early 1990s. Abkhazia claims to be an independent state, but only Russia, Venezuela, Nicaragua, Nauru, Vanuatu and Tuvalu recognise it as such. In practice it is a small extension of Russia, which has a land border on its western edge. Abkhazia's currency is the Russian rouble.

In late June 2016, just a few days after Britain's European Union referendum, I set off for Georgia. It was a strange shambolic departure. When I should have been packing, I was writing to my Member of Parliament urging a new referendum. I washed laundry so late in the piece that I travelled in wet jeans. I have never had such a chaotic start to a journey, but that vote to leave the EU did rather upend my emotions.

I flew from Bristol to Warsaw and then on to Georgia's second city, Kutaisi, carrying with me an email from Abkhazia's foreign ministry promising a visa on arrival in the Abkhaz capital. I arrived at Kutaisi airport in wet, grey weather, but out on the highway in a taxi I knew I was in Georgia. Cowherds sheltering under umbrellas padded along with their cattle on the road from Zugdidi. Georgia wouldn't be Georgia without its omnipresent livestock. The taxi driver told me that he had lost his left thumb in the Abkhazia war, which finally felt more real.

I stayed two nights in the town of Zugdidi for a bit of Caucasus acclimatisation and then headed in a taxi to the nearby border. This must surely be one of the few border crossings left in the world where most of the travellers are either on foot or in horse-drawn taxis, covered wagons which ply their trade between the Georgian and Abkhaz border posts.

There is another unusual touch. On the left side of the road, after the Georgian passport control and before the bridge over the Enguri river which marks the border, stands the sculpture of a black revolver facing towards Abkhazia. But the barrel of the gun is twisted upwards in a knot and this actually points at the sky. While the intention, I suppose, is noble, the sculpture just seems rather odd on this quiet stretch of road.

The Enguri river was in a sense familiar territory. A year earlier I had walked to its source in Svaneti, at the Shkhara glacier, and now I was close to the end of its journey.

Over on the Abkhaz side of the river I came to a solitary passport

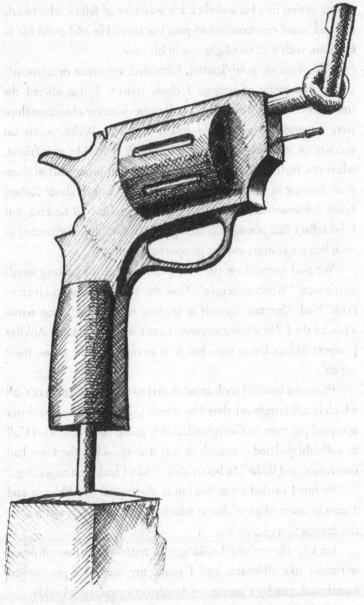

A Georgian peace gesture towards the breakaway region of Abkhazia

officer sitting in a basic shelter. He was a jovial fellow who clearly enjoyed some conversation to pass the time. He addressed me in Russian, with a certain lightness in his tone.

"So, what are you? Tourist, journalist, extremist or terrorist?" Given this menu of options I chose tourist. I also offered the information I was Welsh since the European soccer championships were on and the world had finally heard of Wales, partly on account of its world-class maestro Gareth Bale. My new friend, when not flirting with a passing woman, then proceeded to show great interest in matters Celtic and spoke at length about Robert Louis Stevenson and the Picts. I couldn't follow all he said, but I did reflect that travellers entering Britain would not be treated to such literary conversation at passport control.

We said farewell on the best of terms and his parting words to me were "Welsh extremist". Now the Welsh author and literary critic Ned Thomas, himself a student of Russian, once wrote a book called *The Welsh Extremist*. I can't imagine that my Abkhaz passport officer knew this, but it is strange how he chose these words.

From the border I took another taxi to the nearby town of Gali which is still largely inhabited by ethnic Georgians. The taxi driver accepted payment in Georgian lari. My guide book described Gali as sadly dilapidated – a result of war damage – but the town had commerce and looked in better shape than I had been expecting.

By bus I carried on to Sokhumi, the capital of Abkhazia and a seaside resort of great charm which is finding its feet again after the destruction of civil war.

Luckily the website booking.com marches on into disputed territories like Abkhazia and I made my way to a pre-booked guesthouse, run by a woman of Armenian extraction, Anaida.

Her husband Sarkis, a self-employed mechanic also of Armenian origin, whose forebears fled to these shores after the Genocide, was sitting on a bench in the front yard, pottering with bits of this and that. We fell into conversation. Within less than ten minutes he asked me, "Why don't the English like Russia?" I wanted to say, "Give me a break, I have only just walked through your door!" Instead I said something to the effect that Russia's chequered history, with chapters like the mass murders of Stalin, induced a certain caution in the English where Russia was concerned.

This prompted Sarkis to embark on a list of America's misdeeds over the decades, but happily we did not dwell on geopolitics for long. Still, it was a swift lesson for me that having crossed the Enguri river I was now in a part of the world where the Kremlin's world view prevailed. Sarkis's tone was not one of raw hostility, but nor did it feel like an invitation to amicable open-minded debate on the state of the world.

Partly, I think, the question was simple curiosity on Sarkis's part – in the normal way of things he wouldn't meet many of my compatriots. I spent sixteen days in Abkhazia and did not meet a single person from anywhere west of St. Petersburg.

Sokhumi was badly damaged in the Abkhaz war, but now feels quite prosperous, feeding off a buoyant tourist trade from Russia. Orange and white trolley buses trundle through its streets giving an air of municipal normality and Russian holiday makers throng the seafront promenade lined with oleander bushes. It feels like a good-tempered resort of the old-fashioned kind. During the day a little train takes children for rides along the promenade and in the evening couples come out and dance. Groups set up tables on the stony beach and drink. Young boys shout, "Garyachaya cuckoorooza", which to my ear is more melodious than "Hot sweet corn". I can imagine spending a few happy days shouting "Gar-yachaya cuckoorooza" on the Sokhumi seafront, but the idea of yelling out the English equivalent has no appeal whatsoever.

Occasionally the heavens open and the seaside idyll is temporarily suspended. Once I spent nearly an hour on the seafront huddled inside a popcorn vendor's stall waiting for a downpour to subside.

I arrived in Abkhazia without any firm ideas on itinerary, but I didn't want to try anything too daring. I settled on a plan of walking from Sokhumi to Gagra, another popular seaside resort about eighty kilometres away towards the Russian border.

I set out on a bright sunny morning. I bought a peaked cap and an umbrella in Sokhumi's excellent central bazaar and just walked down to the promenade and turned right. There were bathers in the sea, people on the beach and patches of snow on the Caucasus peaks. I love moments like this, when you simply walk out in fine weather into the unknown.

At the western end of Sokhumi I was reminded of the region's difficult modern history. I came across the first war memorial of my walk – I was to see many others.

"Eternal glory to the combatants of the Sukhumi battalion who fell in the battles for the motherland!" The memorial gave the names of thirty-six fighters, one dead in 1992, the others in 1993. Behind were the ruins of a five-storey red brick building partly covered in vegetation. Presumably one of the battles for the motherland had taken place right here.

This first day of my Abkhazia walk, 6 July, was also the day that Britain published its long-awaited Chilcot report on the Iraq war, so the human propensity for slaughter was hard to shift from my thoughts.

One of the outcomes of the Abkhaz war was the mass deportation of Georgians from the region. Before the war about half of the population of Abkhazia was Georgian and they greatly outnumbered the Abkhaz. In the political and economic tumult surrounding the end of the Soviet Union, relations between the ethnic groups fell apart, with both sides committing atrocities. In the fighting Russia put its weight behind the Abkhaz and more than 200,000 Georgians were forced to flee their homes. Today, Abkhazia's greatly reduced population stands at a little over 240,000.

The loss of Abkhazia and the ethnic cleansing of so many people is the worst tragedy to afflict Georgia since it regained its independence in 1991. The whole dreadful episode, with so much human suffering, brings to my mind a short conversation I had in Tbilisi in the spring of 2015, when the Ukraine conflict and Russia's role in that had been a major world story for months. In the café at Prospero's book shop on Rustaveli Avenue I briefly met Robert Nalbandov, an assistant professor in the Department of Political Science at Utah State University. Nalbandov told me that he had been writing a book on Russian foreign policy under Putin.

"So what is it like," I asked, "to be a neighbour of Russia?" I half-thought I might get a carefully nuanced reply from a cautious academic. But the good professor's response was bluntness itself. "It sucks," he said.

As I walked through Abkhazia it became clear that linguistically this is a seriously Russified part of the world. Russian is the language on everything from billboards to beer bottles, from fridge magnets to menus. It is the tongue you hear most often.

A linguistic map of Georgia published by the Tbilisi-based Centre for the Studies of Ethnicity and Multiculturalism (website csem.ge) shows how beleaguered the Abkhaz language is. Abkhaz, a Northwest Caucasian tongue spoken by about 100,000 people, is restricted to a band of territory more or less following the coast from Ochamchire in the south to Kaldakhvara in the north, a stretch of about 140 kilometres. In the south, Mingrelian, a Kartvelian language related to Georgian, predominates, while in the Kodor valley of eastern Abkhazia there are villages populated by speakers of Svan. The map shows many pockets of Armenian. But what the map doesn't tell you at all is the primary linguistic truth of Abkhazia – the Russian language is king.

I also realised, as I headed north, just how very beautiful Abkhazia is. After about four hours' walking, largely on roads with no sight of the sea, suddenly there was the Black Sea. I had a glorious view of the whole coast stretching to the northwest, with wooded mountains sweeping down to the water and the golden domes of a monastery glinting in the sun on the other side of a bay. I walked the last few kilometres along deserted beaches, sometimes getting my feet wet because the beach was abruptly terminated by rising land. But these were not savage shores and I came safely home to a long straggling village where I found a room overlooking the sea.

The next morning I walked the few kilometres to the golden domes of the huge Novy Afon monastery, established by Russian monks in the nineteenth century. The monastery and its cathedral are popular spots for day-trippers out of Sokhumi. While there were some worshippers, secular tourists set the tone. But it is a very lovely place all the same, with the domes nestling so naturally among the trees.

From Novy Afon I retraced my steps to the main road, past a lake and verdant landscaped gardens, and walked on to Gudauta. This is also a seaside town, but utterly eclipsed by its sisters Sokhumi and Gagra. I checked into a sterile hotel which reeked of the Soviet era. The front door squeaked outrageously and immediately to its left was a building in ruins. In the morning a kitchen babushka dispensed porridge to guests in a rather Spartan canteen.

After Gudauta the road swept inland and was quite heavy with traffic. The saving grace was the lush green landscape, the trees and the mountains. Some of the trees are so big. The elder trees, with their flowers in bloom, are great bursts of white in the landscape, but so high that the lowest flowers are out of reach. The elderflower enthusiast would need a ladder!

On day three I walked as far as the village of Kaldakhvara. I couldn't see any sign of a hotel or B&B so I just went into a local shop and asked the owner, a woman, if she knew where I could find accommodation. "Would a tent be OK?" she asked. I said that would be fine and she made a phone call. While I waited I took stock of what she sold. This was a well-provisioned country shop. It had plenty of Abkhaz wine, but the shelves also boasted Jack Daniels and Amaretto.

Soon a young man arrived and whisked me off to a nearby camp site. Sadbey, a twenty-three-year-old Abkhaz, said his small camp site was in its first season. He was a qualified mechanical engineer and had studied at Sokhumi and Rostov-on-Don in Russia. He said his grandfather had provided him with the land to start a business. Sadbey was charming, hospitable and mentally attuned to the wider world. He has an aunt living in Virginia. Never again can I view Abkhazia as an improbable distant land of which I know nothing!

On day four I rested and read one of Margery Allingham's novels, *Death of a Ghost*. The time always passes agreeably in Ms Allingham's company.

The next day I completed my walk through the heart of Abkhazia and entered Gagra. Walking along roads is not the ideal scenario, but I felt better acquainted now with this corner of the world. I knew the sounds of the Abkhaz countryside – the chirruping of crickets, the tinkle of cowbells and, rather less poetic, the whirr of grass trimmers.

155

For some of my walk from Sokhumi the road had run alongside a railway line. If you ride this line far enough, you arrive in Moscow. Put the other way, you can travel from Moscow's Kazansky station and 36 hours later arrive in Gagra, in the subtropics. I had never thought before about trains leaving Moscow for the subtropics, but when I checked into my guesthouse I discovered that the place practically shuddered every time a train passed. So I have now mentally adjusted my ideas of Russia's railway network. There is more to it than the Trans-Siberian.

I warmed to Gagra. It is a popular resort in a good sense, without pretension and simply very lovely, with lush green hills tumbling down to the sea. If you have been through a north Russian winter, this coast must be a taste of bliss.

I did fall ill in Gagra, with a stomach complaint and the start of a long attack of hiccups. But such is a traveller's lot on occasions. On my last full day before returning to Sokhumi, feeling distinctly below par, I paid for a place in a four-wheel drive to go to Lake Ritsa, one of Abkhazia's star attractions.

I was glad that I raised myself from my sick bed. The trip to Lake Ritsa, up in the mountains, was glorious. Now you might imagine, looking at a map of the Caucasus, that the route going up to Ritsa is a quiet country road. You would be wrong! The road simply teemed with traffic. Russian tourists in literally hundreds of SUVs dotted the countryside between the coast and the lake, taking in sidetracks that go to two spectacular waterfalls. They often stood in their vehicles, did high-fives with passengers in other cars and generally threw a party over a great swathe of countryside. But what countryside! On the drive to Ritsa the road goes through a canyon and you really couldn't wish for grander scenery.

The lake itself is sublime. The waters are light greeny blue and specked with little paddleboats. The backdrop is wooded hills and behind them a line of snow-streaked rocky mountain. This is a very popular spot indeed, but somehow nature accommodated everyone and I didn't begrudge anyone their time in such splendour. Inevitably, Stalin had a dacha here. (You almost didn't need to be told that. You could probably guess.)

Back in Gagra for my final evening I watched a fierce red sun sink into the Black Sea. This is a town of great natural exuberance and beauty.

My little health problem accompanied me back to Sokhumi (I travelled in motorised transport this time) and this meant that I did not stray too far from my bed much of the time. But I did make it to the botanical garden, a well-tended, well-frequented place with shady bamboo groves and soaring pines and palm trees.

After a few days of doing little I decided to head back to Georgia proper. At the border my old friend the passport officer recognised me instantly and we re-entered the conversational realm of matters Celtic, particularly languages.

For the very first time, just minutes before leaving, I had a conversation in English with an Abkhaz citizen. A man in his thirties told me that he had an MBA from the University of Westminster and worked for a hazelnut-processing factory in Gali just down the road. "We export hazelnuts to Russia," he said. I asked how Gali was doing. "We are building, bit by bit." He said it was slow because no outside investment was coming in, but he struck an upbeat note about Abkhazia. "We have stability," he told me.

That, presumably, is where the British Foreign Office would disagree with him. But during my sixteen days in Abkhazia I didn't see anything to contradict him. The region felt pretty stable to me and never once did I feel unsafe.

I unfurled my Sokhumi umbrella and in light rain embarked

CHAPTER 19

To Georgia's Wine Country

The hilltop town of Sighnaghi in eastern Georgia

One of my favourite words in the whole world is "Gaumarjos". I learned to love this word in Kakheti, a region of eastern Georgia famed both for its wine and its tortured history of foreign invasion.

"Gaumarjos" is the standard Georgian toast and it means "To your victory". The emphasis is on the first syllable and you speak the toast with feeling. In this one word of sinew and muscle are fused the celebration of wine as central to national culture and scorn for Georgia's enemies.

If you have been to Georgia but haven't spent an evening rising to your feet again and again, shouting "Gaumarjos" with all the others at table, then you need to return and make a proper job of it. One wine-soaked evening in particular stands out in my memory, but I mustn't run ahead of myself.

After Abkhazia I travelled over to Kakheti by *marshrutky*. I wanted to fill another gap in my knowledge of Georgia. In my earlier travels I had somehow missed the pretty town of Sighnaghi, a few kilometres before the Azerbaijan border and a favourite tourist destination.

Sighnaghi is a two-hour, six-lari ($2.60) *marshrutka* ride from Tbilisi. It is an engaging, hilly town, all cobbled streets and red-tiled roofs. My Lonely Planet guidebook is right – the town, perched high above a plain, has a distinctly Italianate feel. Somebody has had the daft idea of basing quad bikes for tourists smack in the middle of Sighnaghi, but the overall impression is still of a town in beautiful countryside, peaceful but plugged in to the wider world. I found my guesthouse, which faced north with brilliant views of the plain below. Beyond, hidden in a heat haze, were the Caucasus.

My main focus in Sighnaghi was to learn about Georgian wine but first I attended to my health. More than a week after falling ill I still wasn't right, so for the first time in the Caucasus I went to a doctor. No one was waiting so I walked straight into the surgery for a Russian-language consultation with a Georgian doctor. She said I had had food poisoning and gave me instructions on diet. She also prescribed some pills and charged 30 lari ($13) for her time. I got better and was impressed by Georgia's health service.

Before delving into the world of wine I also took in the local museum, which teaches the visitor some of Kakheti's doleful history. Persia's seventeenth-century ruler Shah Abbas I invaded Georgia three times and on his third go devastated Kakheti and took 200,000 captives. The museum says Abbas wanted to take Georgia's farmers and warriors to Iran and to eradicate Georgia as a serious rival in the silk trade.

The museum is something of a shrine to artist Niko Pirosmani (1862-1918). It has fourteen paintings by him, the biggest collection outside of Tbilisi. Posthumously, Pirosmani rose to fame in his native land but in his own lifetime he was poor and generally unknown. The museum strikes a plaintive note when it informs visitors: "Pirosmani passed away in loneliness and obscurity in 1918. Even the location of his grave remains unknown."

Pirosmani's trademark style is primitivist, spare, quirky and infused with a spirit that is all his own. His figures have no expressions on their faces. He was born in a Kakheti village to a family of peasants who owned a small vineyard and some of his art honoured the life of the peasant and the grape harvest.

One painting on display features a peasant in a white belted tunic and black cap, standing with a full basket of grapes in front of him. His wife holds a smaller basket, also brimming with grapes, and to his left is a well-laden vine. Another more ambitious composition shows stages of the harvest from picking and pressing the grapes to preparing for the community feast.

Pirosmani was also fond of painting deer, an embodiment of beauty and spirituality. He kept body and soul together by a succession of jobs such as signboard maker, railway conductor and dairy farmer. Most of his paintings were done on black oilcloth, a medium suited to his modest means.

Today Pirosmani is accorded an important place in the pantheon of Georgia's artistic heroes. The museum describes him as "a live bearer of the 'cultural memory' of his country."

In this role of cultural bearer, Pirosmani celebrated winemaking – it was in his blood and as a good Georgian he knew how vital it was to the land of his birth.

In the words of wine writer Alice Feiring: "Wine is the Georgians' poetry and their folklore, their religion and their daily bread."

In her study of Georgian wine called *For The Love of Wine*, Feiring says that "Georgia, with its 525 or so indigenous grapes, has the longest unbroken winemaking history. They say it has eight thousand vintages."

The Georgian National Museum in Tbilisi has cultivated grape seeds which carbon dating puts between 6,000 and 8,000 years old. Georgia likes to think of itself as the cradle of wine civilisation.

Traditional methods of making wine, using earthenware vats called *qvevri* sunk into the earth, are still used in Georgia. Not only that, but these age-old methods, which provide stable temperatures for the wine, are now finding favour in other parts of the world. Feiring, an American, says the world has gone crazy for making wine in clay pots – France is importing Georgian pots for heaven's sake – and someone is making them in Texas.

With its long history and wonderfully distinctive wines, Georgia has become a kind of super-star in the firmament of natural wine producers. I meet several wine growers in Sighnaghi and they are a doughty bunch of men determined to keep the flag of authentic Georgian winemaking flying high.

I have an introduction to John Wurdeman, an American artist who has settled in Sighnaghi and is one of the business partners in Pheasant's Tears, a small wine producer with a big reputation. Wine connoisseur Dolph Lundgren has described its 2008 Rkatsiteli as "maybe the strangest, toughest, most ass-kickin', car blowin'-up wine of all".

John invites me to lunch at the Pheasant's Tears restaurant in Sighnaghi. When I turn up he is in full flow in Russian, addressing a tour group.

When he arrives at our table business matters are still whirling in his head. "The Latvian ambassador wants to have dinner with me at Azarphesha," he says to someone, referring to one of his Tbilisi restaurants. But he quickly focuses on the conversation with me.

John is a commanding figure, quite stocky, bearded, with a warm smile and an obvious ease in the polyglot world he has created for himself. His wife Ketevan is a Georgian folk singer.

So how did a man born in 1975 into a family of artists in New Mexico end up in Sighnaghi? He says he first came to Georgia in 1995 when he was an art student in Moscow. The draw for him was the music, particularly the Georgian traditions of polyphony. "I first discovered Georgia because of a CD I bought when I was sixteen years old, called *Georgian Folk Music Today*."

In Moscow he started to study Georgian and to hang out with Georgians. Members of the diaspora in Moscow invited him to their country in 1995.

"They whisked me straight from the airport to a restaurant. And I am a vegetarian and being a vegetarian in Moscow in the early nineties was not interesting. And showing up at this feast in Tbilisi and there's all of these small tapas-style mezze plates of gorgeous vegetables, nutted vegetables and roasted vegetables, and then this amber-coloured wine that was being poured freely from the pitcher, toast after toast. I thought I was in artist's heaven. And they summoned musicians to come, about ten, twelve toasts deep into the feast, and the musicians that walked in, they ended up being the same musicians who were on the CD I bought when I was sixteen years old."

"I fell in love with the country on my first trip," said John.

In 1998 he left Moscow for good and came to Sighnaghi to live. He met Ketevan and they married the following year. Gradually the idea of winemaking took shape, after it dawned on John that rural Georgia offered much better fare than what was served in so many of the country's Soviet-style restaurants.

"And so we thought 'What would happen if we made wines that were unabashedly Georgian that could be exported?' – because most of the wines being exported were from big factories that didn't have Georgian soul or character. We would make them organic from beginning to end, we would champion some unusual varieties that were less known like this one – Tsiska – and we would tell the wine story to the world. Very quickly after that we realised that the food component was necessary. We started this place eight years ago."

On Georgian food John talks with deep knowledge and a touch of poetry. After extolling the food of Svaneti – "Svanetian cuisine rocks" – he soon moves to another Caucasus region, Tusheti. "In Tushetian cuisine there is so much more than the average traveller gets. For instance, there are these little gnocchi cooked with caramelised onions and a garlic yogurt sauce. There are cheese pies that are paper thin, that have no yeast in them whatsoever, that use whey as the liquid in the dough and inside they have curds that are dried in the sunlight. Really exotic stuff and Georgians themselves don't even know about it."

Now and then John interrupts his gastronomic tour of the Caucasus to draw my attention to what we are eating. We share many tasty dishes, including delicious oyster mushrooms prepared with yogurt, rosemary, garlic and chilli.

Georgia, he notes, still has many families growing food and selling in farmers' markets. But Georgian agriculture is not all organic. "We

164

are trying to spearhead and push a conscious return to organic farming. And that's, by the way, strained water buffalo yogurt," says John, pointing to one of the dishes filling our small table.

"And this wine here is a very unusual one. It is a rosé Rkatsiteli. So it is actually made from a white grape." John explains that it has had three weeks of "skin contact", meaning that the grape skins spent three weeks in the *qvevri* with the rest of the fruit and the result is a wine that has come out looking red.

Professionally, John keeps many plates in the air. Among other things he is involved in a music school headed by his wife. So I take the conversation to the high ground and ask John, "What is your main thing?"

"Well, in my heart of hearts, what I am still most passionate about is painting, and I do paint. I try to paint for a couple of hours each day."

I ask John whether being in Georgia has given him a sense of having come home. "Very much so. My childhood was in New Mexico and it's a very artistic and a creative place with a good food scene, but – I don't want to say anything bad about America, because there are definitely very good parts – but I never felt at home there."

John discerns what he calls a "certain plasticity", by which he means an artificial, plastic quality, in life in much of the West. He receives chefs and artists of different kinds from outside of Georgia every year and it seems part of his calling is to provide them with a refuge from the inauthentic.

"You can go to a beautiful small town in Belgium, or England for that matter, and you feel that it has been rendered to museum conservation, you know, that it is not a living thing. It is something to look at as a part of the past, that is currently dead, where you can take pictures of it and buy postcards and maybe have tea next door to it, but the idea that a song can be 2,000 years old and people can spontaneously break into it, the idea that an 8,000-year-old vessel is still being used for making wine, and that grape varieties that were almost lost, are all of a sudden reappearing and reclaiming the lands that they are from, that it's an ancient tradition with deep roots that isn't rendered to a corner in a museum, but is alive and kicking – I think that is perhaps Georgia's greatest gift to the outside world. [Western] chefs, the singers, the dancers, they miss that, they are yearning for that. They want food, vegetables, songs that have depth, that quench the thirst of their souls."

John says of Georgia, "It is still not so polished and so veneered that you can't feel the real living culture." He contrasts Georgia, which he calls vibrant, with some of the more battered cultures of Western Europe. "I imagine it is similar in Wales, but you go through Scotland, you go through Ireland, you feel a very proud people that once had a very grand culture, that a shadow of it is still intact and they are holding onto that with pride but, like Corsica the same thing, you feel like it has been so beaten up and so fractured that they can only offer a certain angle of it."

"In Georgian culture, the religion, the language, the singing, the dancing, the cuisine, the viticulture, they are all totally interlocked."

John suggests that the strength of Georgia's culture today stems partly from the historic threat of invasion, which meant "having a sword that needed to be sharp on both sides at any moment".

"They felt that at any given time they could lose their identity, their religion, their language, their ethnicity and they didn't want to take anything from anyone else, but they would fight to the death to protect that which was theirs. That feeling of threat and concern indirectly enabled them to actually retain their culture."

He stresses the need for Georgia to keep its acuteness, to pass

166

on to the next generation the importance of the songs and the winemaking.

"There are easier ways to make wine than in *qvevri*. Our Pheasant's Tears wines are in more than twenty-five two- and three-star Michelin restaurants around the world, including the top two, generally considered the top two, Noma (Denmark) and Roca Cellars (Spain). Both have our wines in their tasting menu. I mean, that's an achievement for an American artist and a Georgian farmer working together."

Pheasant's Tears now sells to twenty-two countries. It produces 60,000 bottles of wine a year from grapes grown on twenty-four hectares in five locations.

John's account of the international success of Pheasant's Tears puts me in mind of UNESCO's decision to place the *qvevri* on its Intangible Cultural Heritage list – basically a UN acknowledgement that the *qvevri* is a jolly good thing. John expands on Georgia's place on the UNESCO list.

"The first thing that was protected as a cultural heritage in Georgia was the polyphony, Georgian polyphony as a masterpiece of intangible European culture. And the second thing was the knowledge of how to build *qvevri* and make wine in them. And this is very important because uniqueness inherently imbues value. In a world of growing globalism you come empty-handed to the table if you mimic others. But if you have your own uniqueness then you bring something new, you make the table more diverse.

"Of the two things that objectively we could say is most unique about Georgia, one would be its wine tradition, its history, the amount of varieties, the method and the vessel itself. The second would be the vast (range of polyphonic music) – there is no country, Steve, on earth that has more than 10,000 complex polyphonic songs that are still practised. If you look at all the different variants of the chants and songs it is huge – the archives, the libraries, the recordings, it is absolutely mind-boggling."

As we talk I learn about another project hatched by John. Pheasant's Tears is teaming up with an organic French winemaker of renown, Thierry Puzelat, to make wine from ancient varieties which will be grown on terraces left over from the twelfth and thirteenth centuries in the south Georgian region of Meskheti.

John is thoughtful on the subject of the double-edged sword that is modern tourism. He says tourism can be used either as a way to fortify indigenous culture and support sustainable farming or it can be used as a way to dilute indigenous culture and support industrial farming which is ecologically not sustainable.

He says mass tourism in seaside resorts destroys coastlines. "It brings in, you know, cheap genetically modified food from the US and Turkey instead of local food. It is a very dangerous thing. Today we are seeing that a little bit already on the Black Sea where you go to Kobuleti and it looks like a poorly done version of a Turkish coastline where there is shawarma and Efes beer everywhere."

I say that part of the customer base for the resort-style tourism he decries is Russia. So are the Russians he meets receptive to the kind of worldview he embraces?

He pours us some 2010 unsulphured Rkatsiteli and expounds on Russia and Russians. "I have no love for the policies of the Kremlin, nor for the bigotry and racism and ambition of Middle Russia, but I do have a huge love for Russian literature, Russian painting traditions and Russian opera.

"The ones that end up coming here are often very curious about natural wine, they are very curious about the dishes that they couldn't get anywhere else, very interested to taste some variety that is unique and it is very refreshing to work with them.

"But I am the last person to focus my businesses [on Russia]," adds John. "I mean, we don't export to Russia, on purpose, because we don't believe in the manipulation that the Russian government uses. Russia uses imports of mineral water, wine and spirits from Georgia as a political weapon and we don't want to be a part of it."

In 2006, when Georgia was moving closer to the West and relations with Russia were deteriorating, Moscow banned imports of Georgian wine and mineral water. These have since resumed, but John is not the only person in Georgia wary of close economic ties with Russia.

It has been quite a lunch – great food, conversation and wine – and I express gratitude to John for his distilled thoughts on many subjects. "Thoughts need decantation, not only wine," says John.

Two days later we meet again. John invites me to breakfast with his Japanese importers at his vineyard close to town, by the village of Tibaani near its sixth-century monastery of St Stephen. It benefits from long summer sun, more than fourteen hours a day, and the soil is lime rock, chalk and dark clay on the surface, with sandy loam and gravel below providing good drainage.

There are two men and one woman in the Japanese group and shortly after eight we sit down with John to a hearty breakfast including a delightful sparkling wine which Pheasant's Tears sells to Noma restaurant in Copenhagen. It doesn't come much better than this!

After breakfast I visit the final resting place of St Nino at Bodbe Convent just outside Sighnaghi. It is a serene place, part of the essence of this little corner of Georgia.

Then at lunchtime I am drinking again, back at Pheasant's Tears for a wine-tasting session laid on for the Japanese. John has invited a Frenchman, Vincent, who also makes wine in Georgia, to come with his wines and all in all we taste more than twenty wines.

The wine writer Alice Feiring, in her work on Georgian wine, enthuses about "sensual explosions of blossom water and honey without the sweetness" and "church-evocative spices of myrrh and frankincense". I am too far gone in my cups to add anything to that. Part of the charm of the occasion is that John, Vincent and one of the Japanese men all speak Georgian and use it for some of their conversation together.

At evening time we are still drinking, having wandered from the home of one winemaker to another. Our last port of call is the home of John Okro, an urbane British-trained telecoms specialist who now makes natural wine. His house is right at the top end of Sighnaghi with great views over the town and the plain below. It is here, over dinner, that we clink glasses and shout "Gaumarjos" again and again. Many stories are told and I will recount just one of them, as related by John.

Some wine experts from the Languedoc region of France travelled to Georgia, to the vineyard of John's business partner Gela Patalishvili. They couldn't believe that he eschewed fertilisers and kept asking him what he used. The first couple of times he ignored them, but at the third time of asking he gave a spirited reply.

John told us, "He stood up and said, 'Every square metre of my vineyard is soaked with the blood, sweat and tears of my ancestors. What the fuck do you use in Languedoc?'"

CHAPTER 20

One Caucasus

The Caucasus summoned me and I obeyed.

Now I am back where I started, at home in Wales, trying to make sense of it all. I fell in love with the Caucasus. I don't want to over-analyse why I love it so, but I have John Wurdeman's words ringing in my ears – thoughts need decantation, not only wine.

Stories need a beginning, a middle and an end and here are my final thoughts to round off the tale – personal musings on a few threads that feel important to me now after my visits to the region.

I knew joy and beauty in the Caucasus – that is the front-page headline. While I can also experience joy at home, I came back to my own hearth feeling emotionally richer and more content. I don't wish to lay upon the peoples of the South Caucasus the allegation that their region is perfect. It is not. But I found it profoundly beguiling and nourishing, a reminder to me of the importance I attach to wild nature and to the life of the spirit.

There is a sense of the sacred in the Caucasus; you feel it in the air and it is a complex and many-layered thing. A deep understanding of spirituality in the Caucasus would probably take a lifetime of study, but what is immediately striking is that this part of the world cleaves to religious belief – and this after seven decades in an atheist empire, the Soviet Union.

When my mind dwells on Caucasus spirituality, I personally tend to think of the Georgian region of Tusheti, where there are Christian churches but also many pagan shrines called *khati* adorned with animal horns. Both in Armenia and Georgia, the world's oldest Christian nations, paganism lives on even today as an element in the spiritual mix.

Falling in love with the Caucasus is a fate that has befallen many visitors. I am not alone! This land of resilient people and awe-inspiring peaks higher than the Alps gets under the skin of many a traveller and never leaves them. It is the polar opposite of bland. Writers, of course, leave the fullest accounts of their passion. One of my main learnings has been the discovery of at least a small portion of the literature inspired by the Caucasus and savouring just how wonderful this body of work is.

Many of the titans of Russian letters have gone to the Caucasus and been shaped by their travels – Alexander Pushkin, Mikhail Lermontov, Leo Tolstoy, Maxim Gorky, Osip Mandelstam, Boris Pasternak and Vasily Grossman come to mind. If you took the Caucasus out of Russian literature it would leave a gaping hole. I wonder whether any other mountain chain in the world has served as such a powerful muse.

Tolstoy's case is particularly striking because Caucasus themes inspired him at every stage in his career, after he volunteered for the Russian army at the age of twenty-three to fight against the Chechens. Even his final novel, the magnificent *Hadji Murád,* is set in the North Caucasus. He wrote it half a century after he first went there in the early 1850s and he wrote it during a period when he spent much of his time penning tracts denouncing fiction. *Hadji Murád,* an almost unbearably moving tale of the horrible waste of war, is one of the masterpieces of world literature.

Such was the pull of the Caucasus for Tolstoy, that after his dramatic departure from his home of Yasnaya Polyana, in the middle of the night at the age of eighty-two, he boarded a train heading south towards the Caucasus. He died at a railway station when his journey had barely begun.

Looking beyond Russian letters, English-language authors too have found their voice after setting foot in these lands. I introduced Englishman Douglas Freshfield as a member of the first team to climb Mount Kazbek. He also wrote extensively, and very touchingly, about the Caucasus. In his two-volume work *The Exploration of the Caucasus*, Freshfield seeks to play down his literary skills and describes himself as a matter-of-fact mountaineer. But Freshfield was so much more than that – he was a writer.

On one of his journeys he travelled through some very remote parts of Abkhazia, entering by way of Svaneti, up to the northeast. In a chapter entitled *The Solitude of Abkhasia* he describes the view in the upper reaches of the Kodor river.

"It was not so much any individual peak that fixed the eye as the glory of the whole landscape – the rolling leagues of forest, the broad hills bright in the early sunbeams, the flashes of light in the depths: here a cliff, there a sinuous reach of river, nowhere any sign of human habitation."

Freshfield makes it clear that for him the Caucasus was a welcome change from the roar of late nineteenth-century London; it was an experience of spiritual solace.

"Men may still, as in past ages, look to the mountains for their spiritual help. In the shining silence of the storehouses of the snow we may find a welcome interlude to the perpetual gloom of our northern cities and the din of a commercial civilisation."

In our own times too, the Caucasus has proved to be a muse. US journalist Wendell Steavenson lived in Tbilisi at a time of economic hardship and acute power shortages in the 1990s. She fell head over heels for the place despite its manifold imperfections and proceeded to write *Stories I Stole,* an electrifying love song to Georgia. It is a non-fiction work of great beauty and her attention to detail is Tolstoyan.

One friend of mine has told me that I have become a Georgian *infatué.*

(I know, this word isn't in the dictionary. But it should be.) I plead guilty and when I read Steavenson I feel I am in good company.

I have heard the view expressed, in my own country, that the Caucasus region belongs to "the periphery", whatever that means exactly. A big part of my learning is that in my gut I know that the Caucasus is not peripheral. It has become important in the contents of my head and I am still on a journey to understand it more deeply.

The Caucasus is evolving and changing and trying to find its place in a turbulent world. So, I would like to look briefly at forces that are pulling the three countries of the South Caucasus further apart from one another and forces that are bringing them closer together.

That same Russia, whose poets have sung the praises of the Caucasus, has been a deadly player in the geopolitical game in these parts and still plays a central role, very much in the spirit of the classic adage "divide and conquer". Travelling through the region, I found that I had to decant my thoughts on Russia. To change the usual metaphor a little, Russia felt always like the bear in the room.

Taking a deep historical perspective, it is clear that Russia has had within it a strong expansionary dynamic. British historian Orlando Figes, in *Natasha's Dance A Cultural History of Russia,* writes: "From the capture of Kazan in 1552 to the revolution in

1917, the Russian Empire grew at the fantastic rate of over 100,000 square kilometres every year." The hunt for lucrative furs first drew the Russians on.

Today, Russia cannot expand in the same way. But this long history of pushing out the boundaries of the empire for earthly gain surely means that it has no model for how to build a friendly, co-operative relationship with immediate neighbours. It has to build such a model from scratch. Several of the countries that have escaped Russia's grasp, such as the Baltic states, Ukraine and Georgia, are not on friendly terms with the Kremlin.

I pick up too another sort of restlessness in Russia's history, a yearning to be relevant on the world stage. At its best, this has been pitched in high-flown, idealistic terms. Fyodor Dostoyevsky, in a speech on Pushkin in 1877, said, "Yes, the vocation of the Russian man is indisputably an all-European and a world-wide vocation. Perhaps indeed to become a genuine complete Russian can only mean (in the last resort, let me emphasise) to become the brother of all men…" In the light of twentieth-century history, these words have a hollow ring. I think Dostoyevsky was sincere and I am left with a feeling that today's nuclear-armed Russia, with its bristling fleets and fighter planes, is still searching for its vocation in the world and is not a happy bear. And this disgruntlement is not good for Russia. Nor is it good for its neighbours or for the world.

I have not set foot in Russia for many years, but the mood by all accounts is sour. There is a feeling of hurt national pride and a suspicion of liberal values. The Belarus writer Svetlana Alexievich, winner of the 2015 Nobel Prize for Literature, told the *Financial Times* in an interview published in June 2017 that sixty to seventy percent of the Russian population hold such opinions.

She told the newspaper: "To be in conflict with the authorities is one thing. We Russian writers have got used to that. But to be in conflict with your own people – that is truly terrible."

One of her themes is the refusal of Russia to look honestly at the bloody legacy of Communism. In her Nobel lecture in 2015 she said Russia was "a space of total amnesia". She told the *Financial Times* that things were now getting worse, with grassroots initiatives "putting up more and more statues to Stalin".

None of this makes Russia an easy neighbour.

One priority for the countries of the South Caucasus is to shape and implement policies towards Russia. When the Soviet Union tottered towards its end there was ebullience, a sense of release. Georgia, Armenia and Azerbaijan had their troubles when the Soviet empire fell and trade links were disrupted, but they all shared a sense of turning a page of history and starting anew.

In the first instance, both Georgia and Armenia moved away from Russia. The Polish foreign correspondent Ryszard Kapuściński was in the Armenian capital Yerevan when the Soviet Union was in its death throes. In his book *Imperium* he writes: "Russian signs, posters, portraits – it is all gone. The city is undergoing a period of intense and scrupulous de-Russification. Many Russians are leaving; Russian schools are closing, as are Russian theatres. There are no Russian newspapers or books. They have also stopped teaching Russian in Armenian schools."

It is fascinating to read this now because Armenia has since done a U-turn and become a close ally of Russia. In Yerevan there are now Russian newspapers, books and theatre. Even more to the point there are Russian soldiers, invited in by the government to provide defence and patrol the border with NATO member Turkey.

Georgia, on the other hand, actually fought (and lost) a war with Russia in 2008 and pro-Russian separatists control a fifth of its territory, to the great chagrin of Georgians. In other words, the two countries have given diametrically opposed answers to the fundamental question, "What sort of relationship shall we have with Russia?" It is true that Tbilisi, since the 2008 war, has sought to improve its ties with Moscow. But there is still a gulf between the Russia policies of the two countries. Today's Georgia aspires to be part of the European Union and NATO.

Looking out for decades, Armenia sees its future in alliance with Russia. In 2015, when I was in Yerevan, I submitted some questions by email to Armenia's deputy minister of foreign affairs, Shavarsh Kocharyan, and he replied on 18 November.

I asked whether the agreement over the stationing of Russian troops in Armenia had a time limit. He replied: "According to the agreement between Armenia and Russia signed in 1995 and according to the protocol on amending the agreement signed in 2010, the deployment of the Russian military base in Armenia has been extended till 2044."

Armenia has agreed to pay part of the cost of the base and this close alliance with Russia is not universally popular. One Armenian woman told me how cross she was that a restaurant in the country's second city Gyumri had a menu only in Russian – Gyumri hosts the Russian 102nd military base. But the alliance is a fact of life. Not only is there a military pact, but Armenia is heavily dependent on Russia for energy supplies such as natural gas and fuel for a nuclear power station.

Now Georgia's leaders want to take their country into NATO. At the very least this would deepen the divide with its southern neighbour Armenia. Mirroring the situation in Armenia, this pro-NATO stance does not find full support in Georgia. I know my guide in Svaneti, Lasha Tkeshelashvili, believed Georgia should have a policy of neutrality. I don't see how taking Georgia into NATO could make the Caucasus or the world any more peaceful.

It doesn't feel like wisdom. In a worst case scenario it could even be a trigger for cataclysmic conflict between NATO and Russia. Extending NATO into the human fault lines of the Caucasus could make even less sense than building nuclear plants in an earthquake-prone zone. Why tempt fate?

The pro-Russian alignment of Armenia is understandable when you look at the world from an Armenian point of view. A century after the Genocide, Armenians still see Turkey as the historical enemy and feel they need Russia as a friend. The Nagorno-Karabakh conflict comes into the equation too in a big way.

Armenians are deeply attached to holding onto this region, taken from Azerbaijan in war, and this attachment means they cannot afford to have Russia hostile to them. Even though it is allied to Armenia, Russia still sells arms to Azerbaijan. Russia is in a perfect position to stir up trouble, were the alliance with Armenia to falter.

I asked the deputy foreign minister about the Armenian government's view of the Russian arms sales to Azerbaijan. He made Yerevan's unhappiness perfectly clear.

"Russia is the ally of Armenia. Our co-operation with Russia includes all the areas, including the military field, we buy weapons from Russia. Indeed, we are not pleased with the fact that Russia also sells arms to Azerbaijan."

One view among students of South Caucasus affairs is that it suits Russia for there to be no solution to the Karabakh conundrum.

"Russia uses the conflict to keep its influence in the region," said a political analyst from a European Union country in Yerevan.

Over the years since the May 1994 ceasefire there have been attempts by the international community to settle this conflict, which still claims lives. But with bigger matters like the Syria war demanding attention diplomatic energy has drained away from Karabakh.

I heard a telling comment from someone who took part in a meeting of the Organization for Security and Co-operation in Europe (OSCE) in Vienna in November 2014. It is the OSCE's so-called Minsk Group which has sought to bring a peaceful settlement for Karabakh. This particular meeting looked at a range of international questions.

"When Karabakh came up, some people left the room and others started texting," the participant told me in a conversation in Yerevan.

The conflict is one huge barrier to better political co-operation – soldiers facing one another on a front line running from north to south at the heart of the South Caucasus make a mockery of any real attempt by governments to build regional unity.

The Welsh call it *hiraeth*, while the Portuguese talk about *saudade*. It is nostalgia, a longing deep in the soul. It struck me on my travels that the people of this region are experiencing more than their fair share of *hiraeth*.

The older people among the ethnic Armenians who now have Karabakh all to themselves long to stroll by the Caspian Sea along the Baku boulevard as they did in their youth. But war has deprived them of that pleasure. There are trenches, guns and bullets between them and the sea – a border as firmly closed as any border can be.

The ethnic Azeris who used to live in Karabakh but had to flee long for their homes and those glorious forested hills. But war has deprived them too.

Ethnic Georgians forced out of Abkhazia during the bloodshed of the early 1990s long for their homes on the Black Sea shore. But war trumped their hopes.

In Yerevan, Armenians look out over Mount Ararat on the other side of the Turkish border and remember that before the Genocide that part of the world was inhabited by Armenians.

One day, on a Yerevan omnibus, a man said to me within moments of striking up a conservation that "all Armenians dream of Ararat."

Too much unrequited longing is not good, but just possibly it can become a fuel for the creation of a better South Caucasus. I know of at least two initiatives that seek to transcend borders and I wish them both well.

The first is the annual One Caucasus Festival, which started in 2014 and brings together musicians and other creative spirits in the Georgian region of Marneuli. The festival's website explains why this region was chosen as venue.

"The Caucasus suffers from many conflicts. The region of Marneuli is a borderland of Georgia, Armenia, Azerbaijan and is known for being a place where many ethnic and religious groups have been living in peace for many years. It is quite unique in the Caucasus which continues to suffer from a range of conflicts and tensions. Our aim is, with the support of the local municipality, to create an inspirational & safe space to foster the meetings and collaboration of young people from the entire Caucasus region."

The website says that funding for the festival is international, with some financial support coming from the governments of the United States and Poland, Warsaw City Hall and the French Institute of Georgia.

The other project that straddles borders is the planned Transcaucasian Trail from the Black Sea to the Caspian. Given the political complexities of the South Caucasus, it is remarkable that brave souls have embarked on this venture. In years to come, this has the potential to be second to none among the great trails of the planet.

The website transcaucasiantrail.org lays out a vision of "a world-class, long-distance hiking trail that crosses the Greater Caucasus and Lesser Caucasus and connects diverse communities and ecosystems, providing lasting and wide-ranging benefits for people and the environment".

Each of the two intersecting trail corridors will be about 1,500 kilometres long and the website says that the work to create these trails will unfold over the next five years.

It lists as one of its aims "improved cross-border co-operation that contributes to the stability in the region".

The trail's website addresses the question, "How will you build a trail in a region with breakaway territories and frozen conflicts?"

The answer: "It won't be easy and it may take many years but we believe it is possible. People have crossed these mountains for centuries and we hope it will become easier to cross certain areas in the decades ahead. By starting to build a trail we would like to help spur more positive and ambitious approaches."

In 2017 this initiative invited intrepid hikers to beta-test sections of the trail, in Svaneti in Georgia and in Dilijan National Park in Armenia.

The spirit of Douglas Freshfield is surely following all of this with keen interest. I salute these projects with all my heart.

Gaumarjos! To your victory.

Acknowledgements

I am indebted to many people for making this book possible.

My Caucasus trip might not have happened at all, if Laurence Purcell had not planted the idea in my mind.

Between them, Nick and Nina Daubeny, Tim Grout-Smith, Brian Hansford, Christopher Johnson, Jonathan Jones, Emily Miller, Antony Parry, Chris Phillips, Ros Russell, Linda Sadiq and Euryn Ogwen Williams provided great encouragement, contacts and advice on reading and design.

In Georgia, warm thanks go to Alexander Janiashvili and Nino Tsakadze for their friendship in Tbilisi; to the "two Lashas" (Tkeshelashvili and Arshaulidze) for guiding me through the mountains and to John Wurdeman for sharing his delicious wine and his stories. Yuri Millarson in Tbilisi gave me the benefit of his pan-Caucasus perspective.

In Azerbaijan, Zagid Askerov and his family invited me into their home, demonstrating that traditions of mountain hospitality are alive and well.

In Armenia, I had the good fortune to find two generous teacher guides – Vahagn Petrosyan in Yerevan and Armen Hovsepyan in Gyumri. Davit Dilanyan in Yerevan helped me to understand the values of Armenia's "independence generation".

My godson Tom Kinsella was a wonderful companion and ace navigator on a long hike through Nagorno-Karabakh.

Carolyn Faulder and Jon Nixon have my deep gratitude for reading the whole manuscript and giving me feedback.

I am grateful to my daughters Megan and Rachel for giving this book the benefit of their artistic talent. They have provided illustrations and map, turning this into a family project.

At SilverWood Books, my thanks to the design team that created the cover and to Emily Heming for shepherding the book through its various stages with great courtesy and professionalism.